WHAT OTHERS ARE SAYING

"*Simple Habits for Effective Parenting* provides 90 excellent Biblically-based tips for parents as they guide their children in becoming responsible and capable adults. Dr. Schroeder's experience in counseling shines through this book offering practical ideas in seven main areas of parenting."
—Josh D. McDowell, best-selling author of over 150 books

"As parents, we want our children to develop character and faith, but many of us aren't exactly sure how to help them do that. Dr. Schroeder gives sound, timeless advice from the Bible on ways you can help your child become the person God created them to be."
—Jim Daly, President – Focus on the Family

"The basis of our cultural problems is family breakdown. Children are growing up without adequate parenting, struggling the rest of their lives for purpose and direction. What a blessing this parenting book is for today! Following Dr. Schroeder's *Simple Habits* can develop healthy character formation. Key to good parenting is 1) Uplifting atmosphere of love and respect; 2) Loving, firm boundaries with consistency; 3) Openness, honesty and everyone working together; and 4) Security of knowing God's presence. You are right on target, Randy, with this practical book!"
—Rev. Dr. David Ludwig author of *Renewing the Family Spirit, The Spirit of Your Marriage, The Power of WE,* and *Christian Concepts for Care*

"Dr. Schroeder provides parents with what they need most: practical, Christ-centered, easy-to-implement, Biblical direction for effective family life. His heart for family success is evident, and his passion to offer effective parenting tools shines through his writing. ***Simple Habits for Effective Parenting*** will bring you joy and confidence as you travel the sacred journey of being a mother or father."
—Rev. Michael Newman, President of the Texas LCMS District, author of *Hope When Your Heart Breaks: Navigating Grief and Loss*

"Dr. Schroeder's newest book, ***Simple Habits for Effective Parenting***, is a wonderful handbook to help parents who truly desire to raise their children with solid Biblical Christian values to help them become confident and faith-filled Christian adults in a world with an abundance of mixed messages. Filled with time-tested, useable, and practical Scriptural wisdom, the counsel of this guide will prove beneficial to any parent or grandparent who loves their children, regardless of their level of experience. Dr. Schroeder has provided an indispensable and handy manual parents will want to regularly consult and put into practice for the sake of their children, and for the good of our future!"
—Rev. Dr. Gregory Walton, President of the Florida-Georgia LCMS District

"Although it may not seem possible, parenting seems to get more and more challenging with every new generation. After 37 years in the ministry of secondary education I have witnessed this constantly evolving challenge! Thankfully, there are resources for parents to help navigate through the journey of raising children. Dr. Schroeder offers incredible insight into many of the most common challenges that parents encounter with their children. Dr. Schroeder's wisdom comes from his vast experience in shaping the lives of not only his own sons but the lives of countless teenagers.

As one of his former students, I now look back with admiration and appreciation for having a teacher and coach who expected the best from his students and players. "Coach" Schroeder genuinely cared about students and ultimately had a powerful impact on my life and helped shape the way I look at my role in the lives of young people.

Through his book, ***Simple Habits for Effective Parenting***, Dr. Schroeder offers guidance on many specific issues that parents face in raising their children. His presentation of effective methods within the realm of education is especially insightful."

—Paul Looker, Superintendent – Lutheran High School Association of Greater Detroit

"Dr. Schroeder's newest work is a great follow up to his initial, ***Simple Habits for Marital Happiness***. While many parenting books begin with the desired outcome and work backward toward attitude and behavior, he intentionally begins with the foundation for effective parenting established in the love, mercy, grace, and forgiveness of our God and builds from there.

As both a parent and grandparent I deeply appreciate his application that accommodates generational attention to principles that have life application. Assuming our own fallibilities, he encourages us to live the forgiven life as examples toward raising responsible decision makers offering practical examples for day-to-day parenting. The book is not crafted as a textbook but, through a series of lessons, as a reference manual to be consulted again and again for effective practices in order to 'train up a child in the way that they should go' through effective parenting. Generations will be blessed by this work."

—Rev. Keith Kohlmeier, Former President of the Kansas LCMS District

Simple Habits for Effective Parenting

SPECIFIC SKILLS AND TOOLS
THAT ACHIEVE EXTRAORDINARY RESULTS IN
RAISING A CHILD

Randall Schroeder, Ph.D.

CrossLink Publishing
RAPID CITY, SD

Schroeder/CrossLink Publishing
1601 Mt Rushmore Rd. Ste 3288
Rapid City, SD 57701
www.CrossLinkPublishing.com

Ordering Information:
Quantity sales. Special discounts are available on quantity purchases by corporations, associations, and others. For details, contact the "Special Sales Department" at the address above.

Simple Habits for Effective Parenting/Schroeder. —1st ed.
ISBN 978-1-63357-382-6
Library of Congress Control Number: 2021931284
First edition: 10 9 8 7 6 5 4 3 2 1

Front Cover Design: Brent A. Cooper – Cooper Creations Graphic Design

I wrote this book to the glory of God!

My purpose in life is to live with a thankful heart each day by serving my Savior Jesus through my writing, counseling, speaking, and teaching. Like *Simple Habits for Marital Happiness*, I pray that *Simple Habits for Effective Parenting* will enhance the lives and relationships of parents and children.

Words cannot express my gratefulness to my loving, dear wife Ginny. I could not have written this book without her help in so many ways, as well as her constant encouragement.

This book is dedicated to our two sons, daughters-in-law, and our six grandchildren. My wife and I are richly blessed with a caring, devoted family for which we are extremely thankful to our loving God and humbly proud.

Contents

ACKNOWLEDGMENTS

I am enormously grateful for the numerous parents who shared their stories of what skills and tools work in nurturing and raising a child. I am also indebted to the many parents who willingly applied these effective *Simple Parenting Habits* to lead and guide their child toward a confident, motivated, and responsible life.

I always appreciate the tremendous support and assistance of Rick Bates and Crosslink Publishing. Thank you to Liana Brooks for her manuscript suggestions. I am deeply grateful to Brent Cooper for his talents and time in designing a wonderful front cover.

+ + + + +

A sincere thanks to you for reading this book! My prayer is that through these *Simple Parenting Habits* you will become extremely knowledgeable about these proven powerful principles that make a significant positive difference in a child's life.

INTRODUCTION

Simple Habits for Effective Parenting is a Biblically-based valuable resource that will help influence a child's heart to become a confident, capable, and self-reliant adult. The most well-known Bible passage on parenting is Proverbs 22:6, "Train up a child in the way he should go [teaching him to seek God's wisdom and will for his abilities and talents]" (AMP) because you want to work yourself out of a job. As a parent, "training" is leading and guiding your child to eventually succeed without you. When you utilize the specific skills and knowledge in this book, there is a strong likelihood that your child will go through life both closely connected to our loving God and living as a responsible adult.

When reading a parenting book, it is important to note the author's credentials as an expert. I gained a tremendous amount of experience from helping parents I have counseled over three decades. In addition, I have spoken to thousands of parents at seminars, schools, churches, Mothers of Preschoolers (MOPS), etc. I was also a Lutheran high school teacher, assistant principal, athletic director, and head varsity football and basketball coach. I earned a Ph.D. in Marriage and Family Therapy, Master of Divinity, and a Master's in Education.

My wife and I have two married sons, who along with their wives, have earned college degrees. We are also blessed to have six grandchildren. When my wife and I have the joyful privilege of caring for our grandsons and granddaughters, we apply these same *Effective Parenting* ideas to positively impact our grandchildren.

When your child was born, you were not given a manual providing you with skills, strategies, and knowledge about how to be an *Effective Parent*. To complicate matters, both parents rarely experienced the same parenting style in their formative years. This leads to conflicting views on what is the best parenting approach when it comes to raising your child.

This complete how-to guidebook has seven chapters and ninety lessons that provide a foundation which can help unite both parents to agree on the most effective way to "train" their child. As you come together through this parenting knowledge, you will empower your child to eventually be less dependent on you and more self-reliant.

This wonderful resource provides specific skills and useful tools for the seven main areas of parenting. I hope to reinforce what you are already doing right and encourage you to learn new ideas and strategies in those areas where your parenting needs improvement.

My prayer is that this valuable practical book will become your parenting manual to influence your child's heart to be a Godly, responsible adult one day. You can read this comprehensive resource from start to finish or select chapters and lessons out of sequence to help you with specific skills in a particular parenting area. *Simple Habits for Effective Parenting* is an easy-to-understand, straightforward guidebook that will give you confidence to create a wonderful relationship with your child as you lead him or her to become a self-assured and self-reliant adult.

I absolutely do not want you to feel any guilt because of mistakes that you may have made in the past. My wife and I made numerous mistakes and wish we could have a "do-over" with some of our parenting words and actions. Let go of your past mistakes and learn through these skills, how you will do things differently in the future. Through Christ's sacrifice on the cross and His glorious resurrection, you are forever forgiven! Likewise as a parent, remember to extend that same forgiveness when your child makes mistakes.

This beneficial knowledge will make a significant difference in every area of your child's life. As you implement this indispensable information, please also give yourself grace because parenting is not a game of perfection. After counseling and speaking to thousands of parents about these *Simple Habits*, parents who put into practice many of these ideas and skills were highly successful in leading their children to become reliable, capable, and Godly adults.

As an *Effective Parent* you can make a profound impact on your child because everything you do and say is extremely important! Although there are challenges for every parent, this guidebook will help you have a rewarding, enjoyable experience raising your child. My prayer is this sound, sensible parenting resource will grant you more confidence and positive hope for *Effectively Parenting* your child.

CHAPTER 1

HABITS THAT MAKE THE PARENTING FOUNDATION

Proverbs 29:18 provides guidance for your parenting foundation, "Where there is no vision, the people perish" (KJV). Thankfully, the thirteen *Simple Habits* in this chapter are essential for establishing a foundational vision for parenting your child.

These parenting fundamentals are the cornerstone of your child's life as you seek to lead and guide your child. Parenting correctly with the clear-cut concepts found in this chapter will keep you purposefully focused.

The parenting process begins with specific goals to develop you as a leader and an example. Understanding the importance of the four foundational "Rs" will help you become a purposeful parent. Like the four legs of a table, all four "Rs"—Relationship, Routines, Responsibilities, and Rules—must be stable and solid. Acceptance, Affection, Attention, and Appreciation are connected to the first "R", Relationship, and provide powerful ways to show love and encourage your child.

There are numerous qualities you want to instill in your child, but I believe that morals based on Biblical values, character, and determination are three of the most important. The last two lessons focus on how to be an *Effective Parent* through desiring obedient decision-making for your child, as well as the three parenting extremes to avoid.

With the thirteen *Simple Habits* in this chapter, you will be able to parent your child to eventually manage his or her own life as a competent, independent adult. Thus, you accomplish a parent's ultimate goal of becoming nonexistent in your supervisory role because parenting is truly meant to be temporary.

1. A Purposeful Parent with a Plan

The Bible encourages purposeful planning: "He will give you your heart's desire and carry out all your plans" (Psalm 20:4 GW). An extremely important parenting plan is for you to fully understand what internal qualities you want your child to possess as an adult. An *Effective Parent* looks to the future by understanding what it will take for his or her child to become a competent, Godly adult.

Benjamin Franklin said, "Living without a goal is like shooting without a target."

I suggest that when there is no vision for the internal attributes you want for your child as an adult, the greater likelihood your child may have a life of struggles. Every great accomplishment in life began with a dream that became a clearly defined goal. You want your child to fulfill his or her dreams and this parenting resource will help you lead your child in a positive direction with his or her goals.

Successful parenting is never accidental but the result of goal-orientation. As an *Effective Parent*, you will lead, nurture, support, encourage, and value your child. At the same time, remember your long-term objective for your child's independence from you, self-reliance, and dependence on God. Having goals of what it will take to move your child toward self-sufficiency and managing his or her own life one day is essential.

As you read *Effective Parenting*, think about the initial goals to aim at as a parent. Examples are: things to say, specifics for building a parent-child relationship, particular parenting skills to implement, things to model for your child, etc. The more exact you are with written goals the better.

Victorious visualization happens for every great athlete. Professional golfers are some of the best when it comes to visualization. They exude confidence by making a successful shot in their mind even before hitting the ball. As a parent, picture in your mind your child being a responsible, Godly adult one day.

Reading this book will motivate you to be a *purposeful parent with a plan*. Much of your child's success in adult life boils down to *Effective Parenting* and you will now possess powerful *Simple Habits* to accomplish that objective.

2. A Leader NOT a Boss

When you are a leader, not a boss, your child will feel safe and secure. Business leaders provide employees with opportunities for growth and success. A leader believes in his or her employee to do the job on their own which brings out the best in an employee.

A boss controls and micromanages his or her employee with too many rules. A boss gives the employee a task and then continually looks over the employee's shoulder dominating the work process. A bossy parent will exasperate the child (Ephesians 6:4). Children do not respond well to a bossy parent, so always lead, never boss!

Parental leadership is the activity of influencing a child by word and deed. To be a leader, your biggest challenge is yourself. Are you becoming more of a leader every day? Every exceptional leader is also a learner. Leaders learn from other people, books, podcasts, videos, and life experiences.

A parental leader is a gentle authority figure who possesses predictable behavior and allows for freedom of choice, NOT control. A parental leader also avoids being a demanding dictator who bosses the child. Instead, he or she establishes expectations to protect and lead the child and fairly, lovingly enforces those limits.

Parental leaders set the example, thus, bringing out the finest in their children. Parents who lead help their child become a competent and capable person. A leadership parent wants the child to manage his or her own life. A leadership parent increases the likelihood that the child will regularly assume age-appropriate roles. The quality of your parental leadership will have a great deal to do with the quality of your Christian walk.

Through ***Simple Habits for Effective Parenting,*** you have the challenge and opportunity to grow as a leader in all aspects of parenting. Be a benevolent leader instilling character and courage in your child's heart. Use your parenting leadership skills to encourage, nurture, and build a solid foundation for your child's life. When your child sees you living an ethical life and making Godly decisions, he or she will trust you and be much more likely to follow your ***parental leadership.***

3. An Example

A parent's example will have the most powerful impact on a child's perspective of life. The clichés are true: Example is not the best teacher, example is the only teacher; and values and principles are more caught (from your example) than taught to a child.

Never take your example for granted!

Live out your faith in Christ by walking the Godly path you want your child to walk. Titus 2:7 declares, "In everything, set them an example by doing what is good" (NIV).

A fundamental truth is to absolutely never compare yourself to others. Revealing your life mistakes leads to comparisons between your child and you as a parent and that is unhealthy for two reasons. First, comparisons produce lower self-worth due to not measuring up. Second, comparisons may also lead to the sin of pride creating a feeling of superiority. Also never compare your children to each other. Instead, encourage Biblical values and help them follow the example of Jesus.

Your attitude also significantly determines the health of your personal life as well as your child's attitude toward life. Developing a wholesome, positive attitude is one of the most important goals you may have as a Christian parent. Since your example often forms the future life of your child, constantly work on maintaining an encouraging, Godly attitude for the sake of your child's maturing growth toward adulthood.

Your attitude also sets the morale for your home atmosphere. Whether it is optimism, pessimism, cheerfulness, moodiness, etc., your child will absorb in some form the family air. The reason is, your actions are speaking so loudly your child can't hear what you are saying, to paraphrase Ralph Waldo Emerson. Your child's disposition will often closely resemble one or both parent's attitudes.

Please recognize being an example is not an on and off process, but a commitment to stay the course every single day, so your Godly qualities become a natural part of your Christian walk. Let your example be something your child wants to imitate for his or her entire life. Parenting is "training" your child to follow your example and incorporate your Godly qualities throughout his or her adult life.

4. Operate at a Higher Level In Every Area Of Life

In Lesson 10, I discuss the importance of identifying qualities you pray your child will have as an adult. Many wonderful attributes are also listed in Galatians 5:22-23, "But the fruit of the Spirit is love, joy, peace, patience, kindness, goodness, faithfulness, gentleness, self-control" (ESV).

Whatever qualities you want your child to possess as an adult, live your life at a higher level than your child in each of those areas. A worthy objective is to hope that your child will attain a higher level in each attribute than yourself.

Perhaps grade yourself in every quality you aspire for your child. An admirable goal is to get a "B" or higher in all the qualities you want for your child.

I counseled parents whose four-year old son lacked self-control and had anger issues. Other family members and his preschool teachers also said he was an exceedingly difficult child. When I asked the father what grade he would give himself in the areas of self-control and anger, he graded himself a "D+" in both aspects. Is it any wonder that their son had struggles? The first goal was to have the parent improve his self-control and anger management through books, counseling, etc.

How can you really expect a "B" grade from your child in the "fruit of the Spirit" or any other qualities if you do not have that "B" grade yourself? When your child needs improvement in a quality or certain area of life, make sure that you are also at a "B" grade or higher because your child will become a close copy of your attitude and traits.

Competent, healthy parents strive to avoid offensive language and have a significant goal to only use Godly, uplifting language. If you struggle using foul language, and many individuals do, make it your highest goal to stop using filthy talk.

As a parent, read personal development books, listen to uplifting podcasts, etc. Associate with Godly individuals who are continually trying to improve their life and maintain a positive attitude. Read the Bible and have regular devotions. Subscribe to personal development emails, inspirational newsletters, or encouraging quotes. Set the example for your child through your own personal development program.

Striving for improvement in the "fruit of the Spirit" and other qualities of life will require effort for you and your child. An *Effective Parent* keeps learning and growing, which is also a significant goal for a child. Hence, be willing to change and improve. Set realistic goals, be patient, and aim for small advances as you lead your child toward internalizing positive, Godly attributes.

5. A Healthy *Relationship* Increases Trust

Your parent-child connection is so essential I devoted the second chapter solely to emphasize that *Effective Parenting* always begins with a *strong relationship*. Psalm 127:3 declares that children are a gift from God and so incredibly special they need to be valued daily. For you to lead your child toward a successful, fulfilling adult life, you must establish a ***strong relationship***. Thus, your number one goal is to do whatever it takes to ensure that your relationship is totally unbreakable.

The four "Rs," *Relationship, Routines, Responsibilities,* and *Rules,* are extremely important, but in order of priority, your *relationship* with your child is your number one priority. Psalm 84:12 says, "Lord Almighty, blessed is the one who trusts in you" (NIV). Throughout the Bible, Almighty God tells us and shows us that we can absolutely trust Him. In the same way, build trust with your child with actions first and then words. Without your child's *trust*, you will probably have a difficult time influencing his or her heart.

When your behaviors and vocabulary are God-pleasing, you increase trust and respect, which builds a very solid parent-child relationship. Being extra polite in words and actions along with praising good choices will strengthen a parent-child connection. Laughing at a child, mocking, or breaking promises will not boost a parent-child bond.

You can utilize all these parenting skills, tools, and ideas, but without a ***strong relationship*** your influence will not be nearly as impactful. When there is a disconnect, your child will likely not be influenced by your parenting but more by his or her peers.

Three important words for a successful relationship with your child are communication, communication, and communication. Your child's self-esteem is built through affirmative conversations because that builds a secure parent-child foundation. Positive conversation is needed daily for a sound, wholesome relationship. The stronger your relationship, the stronger will be your child's self-worth. With a solid connection, your child will respect you, and that will lead to a willingness to listen when you find it necessary to apply rules.

I absolutely believe that a strong ***relationship plus*** an effective application of the ***rules*** will help your child become a ***responsible decision-maker***. On the other hand, if your primary focus is rules, with a minor emphasis on your parent-child relationship, you greatly increase the odds of your child becoming rebellious.

I encourage you to work hard at growing in your faith in Jesus Christ because that is the starting point to strengthening the relationship with your child. Only when your relationship with our Heavenly Father is strong will you be able to enhance your relationship with your child. The more you love God in Jesus Christ, the more you want to serve God by living a life to His glory. And the more your child loves you, the more your child will want to follow your Godly guidance and be a responsible decision-maker in all areas of his or her life.

6. Regular *Routines* Instill Organization

Regular parent-child routines allow for time together and that develops a close bond with each other. Sadly, too many parents and children are often like strangers simply because they do not have family routines. Routines provide a wholesome structure for your child both internally and externally. Depending on your child's age, you may want to help him or her establish a routine, so your child knows what to expect each day and throughout the week.

What are some necessary routines that are important? Although not an exhaustive list, consider the following ideas:

- √ Good morning routine
- √ Mealtimes together
- √ Greet your child with a smile and hug
- √ Prayer time together

√ Bonding bedtime routine

A healthy personal life is discussed in Lesson 52 and regular routines are one way to achieve that goal. Your child needs to witness you having an organized life that provides for your personal success. I have found that *Effective Parents* are those who are personally well-organized in scheduling their time.

A productive person is usually well organized in various aspects of his or her life, which is an important goal for your child as well. When you have a clearly defined schedule, you provide a suitable structure for connecting with your child. A word of caution, please remember that family routines must be "flexible" as opposed to "rigid" routines.

7. *Responsibilities* Establish Confidence

The Bible stresses the benefits of both hard work and laboring together: "The one who plants and the one who waters work together with the same purpose. And both will be rewarded for their own hard work" (1 Corinthians 3:8 NLT). At one time, our nation was an agricultural society that stressed the importance of diligence and great work habits. Children were absolutely necessary on the farm to help their parents handle numerous tasks. For example, children learned how to care for farm animals, till the field, plant and harvest crops, etc. These abundant farming chores provided responsible activities for children. It is not surprising how mature, dependable, and reliable most of those children became as adults.

Likewise, today children need to learn self-discipline through assigned household tasks that are accepted by your child and then reliably finished. It is interesting that some people who were not given responsibilities as children often struggle as adults with feelings of not being capable, productive, and dependable.

It is very detrimental for a parent to limit a child's responsibilities along with his or her decision-making opportunities.

Parents who overcompensate for their children usually foster an unhealthy parental dependence producing children who are often incapable and incompetent to deal with adult life.

One essential parenting goal is for your child to function as a self-sufficient adult. One way to accomplish that task is to provide your child with numerous responsibilities over his or her eighteen years under your supervision. With each stage of your child's development, the number of tasks along with the difficulty of those responsibilities should be increased.

When your child helps around the house, he or she is not only contributing to the family's good, but more importantly, he or she is building his or her self-worth and self-confidence. In the early years, it might be picking up toys and putting away books. During the teen years, those responsibilities might be mowing the grass or washing the car. Children who are given responsibilities by their parents develop a self-assurance that they can succeed in life.

When you give your child responsibilities, he or she certainly sees that as an indication you believe he or she is capable in handling tasks that you ask him or her to fulfill. Completing responsibilities will be one factor in leading your child to an autonomous, competent life.

8. *Rules* Increase Freedom

The Bible provides a foundation for rules to guide a person's life. Jesus summed up the rules of life by stating, "Love God with all your heart and all your soul and all your mind" and "love your neighbor as yourself" (Matthew 22:37 and 22:39 NIV). The Ten Commandments are laws for Godly human behavior. 1 Peter 2:16 states, "Live as free men but do not use your freedom as cover-up for evil; live as servants of God" (NIV). Children should have *freedom within the rules,* which allows them to then make responsible decisions.

Society has rules and laws at the local, state, and national level. There are also rules for adults at work and for children in schools. In a similar way, your child needs rules and boundaries in your home to feel secure and have freedom. Home rules prepare your child to easily adhere to work rules and the laws of society.

What would it be like to not have rules at work or laws in society? Some people do not think societal rules are necessary, but what would it be like to drive a car without any lanes or road rules. Rules and laws actually reinforce our freedom to overcome confusion and chaos, thus, preventing a miserable existence.

In a similar way, when you do not specifically let your child know what is expected of him or her, he or she will probably feel insecure, suffer chronic stress, and experience anxiety. Worse, your child may doubt your love because rules are a sign of care and concern.

As an *Effective Parent*, you need to define your rules whether it be inside or outside your home, and then, convey those expectations to your child. Once you have established limits, a lot of stress will be removed from your home atmosphere. Your child is also more likely to respect you and conscientiously adhere to your rules because there are no surprises. With a clear understanding of the rules, your child will develop self-discipline and be more open to your example and guidance.

A caring home atmosphere allows your child to readily understand that reasonable limits are in place because you love him or her. After speaking with thousands of parents, I find it interesting that when a parent-child bond is strong, having rules is not usually an issue for a child because he or she feels valued and special. When you have rules and expect your child to stay within those limits, your child also develops a sense of identity and becomes a responsible decision-maker.

9. Amazing "As": Acceptance, Affection, Attention, and Appreciation

Your child must absolutely have a daily dose of *Acceptance, Affection, Attention,* and *Appreciation* to feel secure, believe in his or her abilities, and know you always love him or her! All *four "As"* are equally important, so they are not listed in order of priority. I hope you understand how important the *four "As"* are for your solid parent-child connection.

a. Acceptance

Loving your child unconditionally is the ultimate goal for every parent. *Acceptance* is giving your child unconditional love *no matter what* he or she achieves or what mistakes or sins he or she commits. *Acceptance* is absolutely choosing to always value, and never devalue, your child. When your child feels completely loved by you, he or she also has the same feeling that Almighty God totally loves your child as well.

I am not saying you must approve of your child's wrongs, but your child always needs your acceptance, a true belief that he or she will always be your wonderful child. Even if your child does something serious like break the law, he or she needs to have complete confidence you will still love and accept him or her.

When your child chooses to make a minor or major mistake and, after giving him or her a consequence or taking away a privilege, you want to share a message like, "I love you *and* I will always love you *and* I don't approve of wrong decisions." When I sin or make a mistake, that is exactly what our Heavenly Father says to me. Through my faith in Jesus, I have total unconditional love *and* acceptance. God is telling me, "You will always have my unconditional love *and* acceptance no matter what!"

NEVER use the word "but" because whatever you said prior to that is overturned whenever "but" is used. "But" often degrades your attempt to nurture your child. Instead, have run-on sentences and use the word "*and.*"

Many parents don't know how to show unconditional love toward their child. One of the best ways to demonstrate acceptance is to look directly in your child's eyes when you speak positive words that make a significant loving difference in his or her heart and mind. Acceptance is also giving specific praise frequently about your child's wonderful internal qualities.

Acceptance is helping your child always know the foundational fact, "I love you so very much because you're my child." Absolute acceptance of your child truly defines unconditional love and is a *Simple Habit* for your *parenting foundation.* Children who feel unconditionally valued before the age of twelve are more likely to resist peer pressure and numerous teen temptations versus children who do not feel thorough acceptance by their parents.

b. Affection

I define *affection* as verbal and physical expressions of love. Your child wants to feel completely confident you love him or her. When you demonstrate any form of affection toward your child, it provides your child with an internal belief that he or she is lovable. If your child does not receive affectionate love from you, he or she usually gets it from something else that could be harmful or detrimental.

More than 70 percent of individuals I have counseled said they never received *BOTH* verbal and physical expressions of love from their parents. Those adults often shared with me that they now felt insecure, indecisive, and not deserving of an enjoyable life. Lessons 14 and 15 will explain in more detail how to show unconditional love both verbally and physically toward your child, so he or she doesn't have those negative feelings in his or her adult life.

c. Attention

Parenting is about daily connecting with your child which requires focused *attention.* My synonym for attention is *time spent* looking into your child's eyes, dialoguing with your child, or doing an activity with your child. Your child cannot thrive without trust, and focused attention is one of the greatest ways to build a trusting relationship. One of your significant responsibilities as a parent is to build confidence in your child's heart through positive focused *attention*.

Take note, being physically present with your child is *not* focused attention. Due to your job and tasks around the house, I realize that you may feel exhausted, overwhelmed, and perhaps think you just do not have the energy for focused attention. To overcome that mental block, have a goal with specific words and actions you will demonstrate daily toward your child for focused attention. Knowing ahead of time those behaviors for positive attention is one of the most powerful ways to connect with your child so he or she feels unconditional love.

d. Appreciation

The apostle Paul was wonderful at giving abundant praise and *appreciation*. The apostle declared, "Praise the God and Father of our Lord Jesus Christ" (2 Corinthians 1:3 GW), and again Paul said, "I thank my God for all the memories I have of you" (Philippians 1:3 GW).

"Thank you" is important but those two words are an expression of gratefulness for something your child said or did. I define *appreciation* as *praise*, which is more than gratitude or a simple thank-you.

Affirming your child will bestow on him or her a feeling of internal value. *Appreciation* or praise creates positive energy in your child. Praise lifts your child's self-worth. When you focus more on what your child is doing right, instead of what he or she is doing wrong, you have an appreciation mindset.

Always give honest praise, not flattery or insincere appreciation. Written notes of appreciation can be even more meaningful because those short notes of encouragement can be reread by your child over and over.

10. Three Qualities to Strengthen Within Your Child

How do you picture your child as an "adult" at twenty-five years of age? That mental picture will help you identify meaningful internal attributes for your child.

Ask yourself: What do I pray for in terms of my child's Christian life journey? What will his or her attitude be like as an adult? What internal character qualities will he or she possess for succeeding in life, as well as handling the challenges of daily living? What important characteristics will my child possess for enhancing adult relationships?

You absolutely need to envision your child as an adult to know how to lead your child toward incorporating positive qualities. There are numerous characteristics that are essential for healthy living, such as "...love, joy, peace, patience, kindness, goodness, faithfulness, gentleness, and self-control" (NLT Galatians 5:22-23), as well as selflessness, humility, seeking good in others, forgiving spirit, willingness to serve, trustworthiness, compassion, etc. I pray that your child will possess all those positive attributes. What will help your child cope with life and succeed as an adult are *three significant positive qualities*:

- Morals based on the Bible
- Character
- Determination

a. Morals Based on the Bible

Your child deserves to have well-defined, distinct values of Godly behavior to follow in life. The Bible instructs all parents, "These commandments that I give you today are to be upon your hearts. Impress them on your children" (Deuteronomy 6:6-7 NIV). Unfortunately, for many people the Bible is no longer the moral compass of society today. In 1980, the Supreme Court took the Ten Commandments out of public schools. Since that decision, the boundaries with sin began being pushed further and further apart.

Solid Biblical values and a stable nuclear family have continued to decline because of many within society moving away from God. Hence, morality has become extremely blurry and left up to an individual's feelings, not Biblical guidance. Such unhealthy thinking leads to the immoral, selfish belief—"If it feels good to me, even though my actions may not be Biblically based, I will choose those damaging behaviors anyway." Such corrupt, worldly thinking would be very detrimental for your child.

The importance of a moral education is reinforced by the words, "Train a child in the way he should go and when he is old he will not turn from it" (Proverbs 22:6 NIV). Do not take a chance by leaving your child to develop morality and faith in Christ on his or her own. Equally important, incorporate Biblical values through your own words and behaviors.

Teach the Biblical absolutes of right and wrong and attend a church that believes in those same Biblical principles. Nothing will confuse your child more than if your actions do not match the Biblical values you are trying to teach him or her. Biblical morals will motivate your child to love God with all his or her heart as well as love his or her neighbor.

b. Character

While morals are the absolutes of right and wrong according to the Bible, *character* is all the internal assets that assist your child in following those ethical standards found in God's Word. Internal Godly character is best seen through external actions because one's core character will become the sum of the choices made that eventually become habits. Having Godly character will help your child make moral decisions.

The Bible talks about the character of God as loving, compassionate, just, good, and holy, to name a few traits. Jesus was patient, loving, obedient, caring, and forgiving. Jesus served the people around him and sacrificed for them.

Character involves ethical functioning by taking action that is consistent with Biblical beliefs. Godly character means doing what you say you will do, practicing what you preach, walking the talk, and having your actions be consistent with your words which equals integrity. Strong character within your child now creates a high integrity adult later.

Being humble is to be teachable and willing to learn, while boasting is a function of sinful pride. Proverbs 11:2 declares, "When pride comes, then comes disgrace, but with the humble is wisdom." Humility within your child is an essential goal because many Godly traits flow from that character quality. A person or child with high character is humble, not needing to advertise his or her wonderful attributes.

Frequently today, the focus for character development is more on feelings rather than absolute Biblical values that make a difference in the lives of people. When an adult or child is making poor decisions, it is often the result of cracks in one's character. Your character will often determine your child's future character. Building character within your child will also strengthen his or her core identity of who he or she is in God's eyes.

A person with *character* will still have weaknesses for he or she is not perfect. However, in the midst of being human, a person with solid character consistently stands for what is right and does what is right in the eyes of God. Hence, develop Biblical character within your child so he or she will be motivated to serve God and others.

I hope the knowledge found in *Effective Parenting* will help you develop Godly character in your child so he or she will succeed in adulthood. I encourage you to identify and write down ten character qualities that you believe are essential for your child. Then, compliment, encourage, and reinforce those character qualities when your child demonstrates a particular positive trait. Beginning today, take dead aim at reinforcing the Biblical qualities you desire for your child's character.

c. Determination

Throughout your life and my life, we have been knocked down, had setbacks, and dealt with many unfair circumstances. Adversity happens to everyone and your child will face hardships as well. Ask any successful person if he or she had misfortunes and he or she will respond with a quick, "Yes, many." The apostle Paul said, 'We know that suffering produces perseverance (determination); perseverance, character; and character, hope" (Romans 5:3-4 NIV). The truth is, most of a person's character is established early in life. Adversity can help build your child's character so that *determination* is also part of his or her personality make-up.

Attitude means everything in terms of how your child will handle adversity. Charles Swindoll said, "Life is ten percent what happens to us and ninety percent how we react to it." Like Pastor Swindoll suggests, I am confident you want your child to react positively and be self-assured that he or she can overcome any obstacle. To have that optimistic attitude, you will want to lead your child to have a persistent, *determined* spirit that causes them to *never give up*!

Winston Churchill gave a commencement address about his philosophy of life. Churchill simply stated, "Never, Never, Never Give Up!!!" That might have been the shortest commencement address ever, but he expressed succinctly an essential attitude for your child. *Determination* is being persistent to never give up!

Extracurricular activities can help your child learn the valuable quality of determination. After your child begins an activity or sport, never allow him or her to quit until the activity is completed. I have counseled numerous adult individuals who shared when they were younger, they quit an endeavor. That established the bad habit of simply giving up in the face of a challenge. Now, when there is any life obstacle, it is that much easier to quit. Whether music lessons, swim lessons, karate, etc., have your child finish the activity or sport he or she agreed upon to solidify a determined spirit.

When adversity occurs for your child, let him or her know that will happen over and over throughout his or her life. Every setback is a great teaching opportunity, but you must be an encourager, cheerleader, and supporter to assist him or her in successfully handling each and every challenge. Reframe adversity, setbacks, or even failures as "new beginnings," "fresh starts," "opportunities for renewed effort," etc. Tell your child: "I believe in you!" "I know you can do it!" "I am proud of you!" "All successful people have adversity and setbacks, and you will be successful." "I am confident you will bounce back!" Think of your own reframes and phrases so your child never gives up and consistently stays determined!

Successful people are just ordinary people with an extra amount of determination. Individuals who think of themselves as victims are satisfied with excuses. Victors say "no excuses" while looking for solutions to the problem. Excuses are simply not an option for a determined person, including your child.

Help your child learn to welcome difficulties with a persistent confidence. When your child never gives up and always bounces back, he or she will not only handle adversity well, but also be a successful adult.

11. Mutual Respect

A foundational principle for all relationships, including parent-child, is *mutual respect*. As the Bible emphasizes, "So then, in everything treat others the same way you want them to treat you" (Matthew 7:12 AMP). Mutual respect is critical for healthy parent-child functioning, as well as essential for your child's interactions with others.

It is essential that your child respects you, not to help you feel good but because you can only influence your child's heart when your child respects you. You will have great difficulty applying consequences and taking away privileges when your child does not respect you. Responsible, good decision-making children are usually raised by parents they love and respect.

Respect is a two-way street. One of the best ways to teach your child respect is to show him or her respect because respect must be earned. Attaining respect requires that your tone of voice and attitude be the same with your child and family members at home just like it is when you address others.

Without respect for you, it is also highly likely that your child will not respect his or her teachers and other authority figures. When a child does not respect his or her parents before the age of twelve, the probabilities increase that he or she may not respect others as a teenager and later as an adult.

What causes disrespect? Disrespect happens when a parent does not listen well, disregards a child's questions, is sarcastic, does not spend time with his or her child, or does not effectively discipline the child.

When a child sees his or her parents not demonstrate respect for government officials, police officers, their pastor, or their boss, a child learns to disrespect authority figures as well. Sometimes, when a parent gives a flippant response rather than a thoughtful reply, it can come across as disrespectful.

Recognize that for your child to respect your Biblical values as a teenager and adult, he or she needs to respect you during the elementary years. Always treating your child as you would like to be treated enhances mutual respect. Be a constant example of *mutual respect* by demonstrating respect, care, kindness, and compassion toward everyone.

12. Obedience Leads To Responsible Decisions

Colossians 3:20 provides guidance for every *Effective Parent* declaring, "Children, obey your parents in everything, for this pleases the Lord" (NIV). Our Heavenly Father wants every adult child of God to also be obedient. Thus, our loving God never controls our choices but seeks *obedience*. Your goal as a parent is to help your child grow in responsible decision-making through obedient choices.

Have your child follow the example of Jesus who "humbled himself and by becoming obedient to death—even death on a cross!" (Philippians 2:8 NIV). Christ obediently paid for the sins of the world offering eternal life in Heaven for all who believe in Him.

With Adam and Eve, our Heavenly Father sought obedience, *not control,* over their decisions. Certainly, the Creator of this awesome universe could have controlled or prevented Adam and Eve from eating the fruit on the tree. However, God wanted Adam and Eve to *obey* and make a good choice. Due to a rebellious spirit, Adam and Eve made the sinful decision to disobey God by eating the fruit.

Many parents believe their number one goal is to control their child's behavior, but that is certainly **not** *Effective Parenting.* Unfortunately, parents who "control" their children may create kids with poor decision-making skills, low self-worth, struggles with perfectionism, irresponsible behaviors, eating disorders, anxiety, depression, etc.

As an adult, how would you like it if someone controlled almost all your decisions? You would probably feel miserable, anxious, and depressed. You do not want your child to feel that way for eighteen years under your roof.

Although not healthy, to a degree it is normal to wish you could control most of your child's life until he or she is eighteen. However, after the age of twelve, when your child is not always around you, your child will start making impactful decisions about smoking cigarettes, alcohol, marijuana, other drugs, academics, and sexual activity.

Children who have learned to make good choices by following a parent's rules and obeying God's laws up until the age of twelve are usually fairly responsible decision-makers during the teen and early adult years. On the other hand, children who were controlled by their parents, may take freedom of choice to an extreme during the teenage and young adult years by often committing irresponsible actions and even choosing to be defiant. When your child has the freedom to make good choices, you are not controlling but helping him or her learn obedience.

An *Effective Parent* has tremendous faith in the child's ability to govern his or her own life. While under your care, the letting-go process can be scary, but it is essential. Your goal as a parent is to help your child become a self-sufficient decision-maker, so that by the time your child is a senior in high school, he or she is making almost all his or her own choices with your guidance. Hopefully, after high school, your child will either go to college or get a job and move into an apartment. As a young adult, responsible decision-making will now be essential!

God wants everyone to obey Him and make healthy decisions because that leads to freedom and a joyful life. Likewise, children who learn *Godly obedience* are also the happiest children, and parents who seek obedience for their children are the happiest parents. Learning obedient decision-making is at the heart of a healthy parent-child relationship.

13. Avoid Parenting Extremes

Maintaining a balance between seeking obedience for responsible decisions and avoiding the "three extremes" is a continual struggle for all parents. When a parent is controlling, overprotective, or permissive, the child usually struggles and is often labeled a disobedient child. It is always important to avoid extremes in parenting your child.

a. Controlling

A controlling parent dominates the child with fear, manipulation, passive-aggressive anger, and strictness over the child's life. The child and the other parent often walk on eggshells trying to fulfill all the rules every day. The controlling parent is the most powerful parent because in his or her eyes, "he or she is always right and has all the answers to life." A controlling parent often personally struggles with anxiety, perfectionism, compulsions, feelings of inadequacy, and low self-worth.

A controlling parent is usually focused on how the child appears to others because a lot of his or her self-worth stems from the child's appearance and accomplishments. On the other hand, an *Effective Parent* has the goal of a long-term perspective of how a child will live for God from the ages of eighteen to one hundred.

A controlling parent is similar to the Pharisees of Jesus' day. The Pharisees had 613 laws or rules that everyone was expected to fulfill. The Pharisees viewed themselves as superior and in charge of others, just as a controlling parent is also in total command of the child. Jesus even said to the Pharisees, "Woe to you, blind guides" (Matthew 16:6)! Sadly, a controlling parent is often "blind" to his or her ruling ways and how detrimental this extreme is for the child.

This extreme parenting style does a great disservice to a child in so many ways. A child raised by a controlling parent will often be defiant and rebellious as a teenager. Or he or she will obey the rules while at home, but after high school, when he or she is making independent decisions, his or her life is wild, carefree, and occupied with party, party, party.

Years ago, I counseled a young man who was salutatorian of his high school class but flunked out of college after his freshman year. Both his parents were loving Christian people.

Unfortunately, their excessive loving ways led to a controlling parenting approach. Through his senior year of high school, these parents made most of their son's decisions for him.

Sadly, when he went away to college, he was unable to decide upon a regular sleep schedule, when to study, how often to go to class, unable to make wise decisions, causing him to fail most of his classes. A truly distressing outcome, but thankfully, it was temporary. His parents and I worked together to assist this wonderful young man to learn how to become a *responsible decision-maker on his own*. He not only earned his college degree but did so with honors.

A controlling parent has a legalistic parental belief system, unbending limits, and a super strict style. This extreme parenting style is almost *all limits with no freedom*. A controlling parent will often express anger in a passive-aggressive manner. Hence, a child has a difficult choice, to live by the rigid rules or experience the parent withholding love in various ways.

Many years ago, I counseled a pastor and his wife who were having significant difficulties with their twelve-year-old son. I lovingly suggested that the pastor's parenting style was strictly rule-focused and his relationship with his son was only secondarily important. I asked this pastor to consider that explanation why their son did not respect him and continually made poor decisions.

The pastor replied, "Dr. Schroeder, you are a pastor and yet you don't know the Bible very well because one commandment declares, 'Honor your father and mother.' My son and our other children must obey my rules even if my relationship is weak." My response to this pastor was, "Your children are to honor you, but they may not respect you. The Bible also says, 'Fathers (mothers), do not exasperate your children' (Ephesians 6:4 NIV).' And to have a rule-focused home without the foundation of a strong relationship will only build a wall, anger within your son, and continual emotional distancing."

Over the course of counseling, I learned his wife was also afraid of him and lived in fear of his marital rules. Thankfully, my statement got the pastor's attention and he made significant positive parenting changes in so many ways. The result was a stronger relationship with his son and a much happier marriage.

Unfortunately, too many loving Christian parents practice this extreme parenting style. Our loving God does not control, so do not ever control your child's behavior. If controlling has been your extreme style, I pray you will be able to open your eyes to the more productive parenting system of helping your child learn *obedience,* which God also desires. Please remember that your *parent-child relationship* is always most important!

b. Overprotective

Some loving parents try to protect their child from all bumps and bruises in life. No devoted parent wants to see a child experience the challenges and heartaches of life. When a parent overprotects, he or she may damage the child emotionally as well as prohibit his or her child from learning personal strength and self-confidence. The more a parent overprotects, the less competent a child feels in coping with life struggles. An overprotective parent will benefit from considering the adage, "What doesn't seriously harm my child will make my child stronger!"

Overprotective parents often had one or more painful experiences as a child that crushed their spirit to the point of emotional exhaustion, anxiety, or even depression. As a result of these unhappy events in their childhood, they overly compensate for any emotional or physical pain that their child experiences. Always understand that it is enormously damaging to overprotect because you negatively reinforce your child to be dependent on you. The detrimental result from overprotection will often be insecurity, immaturity, low self-worth, and stifled growth in your child becoming an independent adult.

An overprotective parent often creates fear in the heart of the child, conveying the belief that "you cannot handle the world or your problems without me." Overprotective parents unintentionally make their child dependent on them, especially when he or she faces difficult times. Continual overprotection fosters a sense of incompetency and feelings of inadequacy in a child.

An overprotective parent is usually also overinvolved in the life of the child. There is an incorrect sense of being indispensable in helping the child survive and even enjoy life. Overinvolvement smothers a child's independence and squeezes the breath out of his or her personal freedom. Overinvolvement is meeting a parent's needs rather than doing what is in the best interest of the child.

An overinvolved parent nurtures an unhealthy dependence. Overprotective parents often produce adult children who struggle with:

- Emotional problems
- Being a people pleaser
- Indecisiveness
- Eating disorders
- Compulsive spending habits
- Alcohol and drug issues
- Other addictions

Please understand most behaviors have a purpose. For example, a child's tears have both a positive and negative purpose, either constructively expressing genuine pain or detrimentally just being manipulative. Unfortunately, rewarding unhealthy tears is easy to do, especially for an overprotective parent. Too often, some parents become overly concerned with their child experiencing minor hurts when they really should ignore the cries. A child may use crying to underhandedly manipulate a parent to overreact and "desperately" respond to a petty pain.

Whenever a child receives a physical injury, his or her crying may come from true physical pain or he or she may shed tears to manipulate an overprotective parent. Letting a child handle physical bumps and bruises on his or her own is one way not to be overprotective.

The next time your child experiences any kind of physical hurt and starts crying, ask your child to come over to you for comfort. When he or she can easily stroll toward you for consolation, you know he or she is not seriously injured, and the tears had the behavioral purpose of getting you to overreact.

Effective parents avoid the extremes of being overprotective and overinvolved by *not holding their child too tightly.* Cuddle-yes . . . coddle-no. Cuddling is nurturing through physical affection, which is beneficial emotionally and physically. Coddling is pampering excessively which is detrimental for children older than three years of age.

Coddling is for babies and toddlers under three, but coddling older children disables their personal internal strength and weakens their capabilities to cope with life challenges, an essential life competency. Continually rescuing a child from every bump, bruise, and pain weakens his or her tolerance for frustration and diminishes a child's ability to stay determined and never give up.

c. Permissive

Another extreme is the permissive parenting approach, where there are simply few rules and few limits. In a permissive home with few limits, children can do almost anything they choose to do. A healthy parent-child relationship is often missing in a permissive home because there are infrequent connections between parent and child. This lack of a relationship often creates a significant absence of respect by the child for his or her parent. Children raised in a home without rules are often irresponsible, rebellious, and unresponsive to any adult authority.

Rarely is the permissive style prevalent in a Christian home. Christian parents usually struggle more with being controlling or overprotective.

Sometimes a parent striving for *obedience* can also be permissive. This type of permissive parent can have a very loving *relationship* with his or her child, have appropriate rules but *not enforce the limits* by being too lenient. Through my counseling of parents and speaking to parents, I have known many individuals who were ineffective parents because they did not successfully apply the rules they had established with their children. These parents often had fair, reasonable rules but they were not decisive and consistent in applying those rules.

By way of example, let us say every day on my street I drive 55 mph even though it is a 35 mph speed limit. I do this daily for weeks, then, one day, a police officer pulls me over but only gives me a warning without a financial fine. Am I likely to adhere to the speed limit? This is a simple illustration of not enforcing the laws (rules). I definitely would have no fear of speeding because there are no consequences.

Wonderful Christian parents often take the same approach with their children. A few examples: A child is late for curfew over and over but there are never any consequences given. A child does not do his or her homework but is still given privileges each evening. A child is disrespectful but never expected to change that defiant behavior. Hopefully, you see how this is a form of permissiveness even though there are rules.

Parents with few limits may do so for many reasons:

- They are not sure how to set boundaries.
- They do not want to upset their child for fear of hurting his or her self-esteem.
- They want to be friends with their child rather than lead and guide their child toward responsible adulthood.

- Due to low self-worth, they simply don't have the strength to apply consequences.
- They just don't see the long-term consequences of not applying limits throughout a child's life.

A child raised by a permissive parent is likely to be rebellious and often angry. Limits are truly welcomed by children! Loving rules and healthy boundaries actually diminish defiant feelings because rules indicate care and concern by a parent.

Thinking of "peas" and "spaghetti" on a plate can easily explain the extremes of overinvolvement and permissive parenting approaches. Overinvolved or overprotective parents are enmeshed with their children like spaghetti on a plate. Each spaghetti strand is entwined and entangled tightly together. A permissive family is like peas on a plate where each pea is not touching and there is not a sufficient connection. Strive for a healthy balance between these two extremes.

An *Effective Parent* wants to maintain a proper balance of involvement by aiming to not be enmeshed with his or her child nor be disconnected. My prayer is that your ***strong parent-child relationship*** coupled with you ***consistently applying the rules*** will help your child become a ***dependable, responsible*** adult one day.

CHAPTER 2

HABITS THAT BUILD A STRONG RELATIONSHIP

The best Biblical example of unconditional love is the father of the prodigal son (Luke 15:11-32), who is also an example of our Heavenly Father's unconditional love for His children. Almighty God always accepts and loves His dear children. 1 John 4:10 affirms God's wonderful love, "This is love; not that we loved God, but that he loved us and sent his Son as an atoning sacrifice for our sins" (NIV). God showed His love through His actions of sending a Savior Jesus from sin, and parents also need to *show* their love daily. Your child should be absolutely assured God loves him or her unconditionally. He or she will never embarrass God, never be rejected by God, and in our Heavenly Father's eyes, he or she is special.

The ten *Simple Habits* found in this chapter are building blocks for enhancing your parent-child connection. No parent will ever be perfect in showing his or her love through these ten bonding ideas. Yet, the more you show love with these ten *Simple Habits*, the better your parent-child relationship will be, and that plays a significant role in helping you influence your child's heart toward becoming a good decision-maker. Daily *show* your love through these words and behaviors that produce a respectful, trusting parent-child relationship.

Your child's deepest need is love, and most importantly, unconditional verbal and physical love. Daily demonstrate your unconditional love for your child in many ways. Your child needs to be confident our ***Almighty God loves them no matter what*** and ***you love them no matter what***! Your child will not care what you are trying to teach him or her, unless your child knows how much you care and love him or her.

I believe your main objective as a parent is to build a *strong relationship* with your child. The stronger your relationship with your child, the more open and accepting your child will be to your parental guidance.

Every parent, spouse, and person would agree that communication is the very best way to build solid relationships. Your home atmosphere includes verbal and nonverbal communication. Both are significant factors in determining your child's life choices. All communication with your child will either value or devalue him or her. This chapter describes in detail what meaningful parent-child interaction looks like. Per Lesson 14, verbally expressing unconditional love is an absolutely essential goal. Equally important is *showing* a child love through the ideas in Lessons 15 through 23.

14. Unconditional Verbal Love

Throughout the Bible, God tells of His everlasting love. God's love in Jesus Christ gives Christians an everlasting confidence, as Romans 8:38-39 affirms, "For I am sure that neither death nor life . . . will be able to separate us from the love of God in Christ Jesus our Lord" (NIV). Likewise, as a parent, tell your child every day that you love him or her. Always ensure that your verbal love statements are genuine and come from your heart. "I love you" statements that are flippant or sarcastic are more emotionally damaging than if you did not utter those words at all.

Words can make us healthy, just as words can make us emotionally sick! Daily expressing unconditional verbal affirmations makes a significant difference in your child's self-worth and self-confidence. Every day, when you honestly speak valuing words, your child will have no doubt you undeniably always love him or her. Saying "I love you" several times a day will also never lose its effectiveness.

This lesson lists in order of value five confidence-building ways to express your verbal unconditional love for your child. Use the meaningful phrases below as ways of expressing your unqualified love on a daily or, at a minimum, regular basis.

I Will Love You Even More Tomorrow Than I Do Today

Every day, and especially before your child falls asleep, share those important words. How do you think your child will feel when his or her head hits the pillow? Unbelievably loved by you! A feeling of security, safety, and comfort will fill every space in your child's heart.

How would you feel if every night before you went to sleep our Heavenly Father would audibly say to you, "I will love you for eternity!" What a tremendous confident feeling it is to know the love of God never ends! You would sleep great, look forward to the next day, and have assurance of spending everlasting life in heaven with Almighty God. Your child experiences a similar feeling of boundless love when you say, "I will love you even more tomorrow than I do today!"

Do You Want to Know a Secret? I Love You No Matter What!

The three most important words in this statement are NO MATTER WHAT because we all want to be loved unconditionally.

The Bible declares through the forgiveness found in Jesus Christ; God loves you no matter what sins you have committed. The knowledge of unconditional love by God is tremendously reassuring and uplifting as we approach each new day.

Almost every time my wife and I see our grandchildren, we ask them, "Do you want to know a secret?" After hearing the question and our answer hundreds of times, before we can say anything they quickly respond, "You love us no matter what and you will love us more tomorrow than you do today!" Sometimes our grandchildren pretend they are tired of the question, but they truly love it.

Your child may also act like he or she wants you to stop asking the question but, in his or her heart, your child definitely desires to hear daily those words, "I love you no matter what and I will love you more tomorrow than I do today!!!" Your child must absolutely know without a doubt that you love him or her unconditionally even when he or she makes mistakes.

I Am Proud Of You

Sadly, I have had hundreds of children ask me, "Dr. Schroeder, do you think my parents are proud of me?" The reason for the question, unfortunately, too many parents rarely say those words. It is best to say those words when your child is not accomplishing any task but just being your child. When your child is riding in the car with you, that is an excellent opportunity to say, "I am proud of you!" This is not empty praise but expressing a joyful feeling due to your immense love for your child.

Why Do I Love You?

Upon hearing this question, your child will often want to answer with something he or she did or said. What a great feeling your child will have when you proudly share the unconditional love statement, "I love you just because you are my child" or "You are so special to me" or "You are absolutely a wonderful child!"

You Are So Very Important To Me

Make simple loving statements to your child like, "You are so important to me!" or "I am so very glad that you are my child!" or "I am so thankful to God that you are my child!" or "You mean the world to me!" or "You are God's gift for me!"

Please realize in the back of your child's mind, he or she has ongoing questions, "Do you love me no matter what?" and "Do you love me at all times?" Your loving words are extremely powerful in helping your child feel good on the inside! Please use these five verbal methods daily to keep your child's emotional tank full and his or her inner confidence strong.

15. Unconditional Physical Love

Every child and person, no matter the age, benefits from touch because we are hardwired for physical affection. Jesus often used touch for healing as mentioned in twenty-two Bible verses. Touches that frequently occur throughout the day will enhance your child's self-worth and self-confidence. Be intentional with your unconditional physical love for your child!

Every morning when you or your child departs, give him or her physical touch, and do the same when you reconnect in the evening. Physical affection and verbal unconditional love are two of the most priceless gifts you can ever give your child.

At times, some children will shy away from touch. One reason they may not like being touched is because of sensory issues. Physical touch always needs to be given in a loving way that acknowledges the needs and fears of the child.

When a child is reluctant, perhaps give physical touch when he or she is involved in an activity like watching TV, reading a book, or playing a video game. You can give the child brief, light touches on the back, arm, shoulder, head, and he or she will receive the touch without complaint because the child is focused on something else. With a child who is reluctant to be touched, take baby steps by increasing the amount of physical affection with each passing day, but do not stop touching your child.

A lack of physical touch may create a real insecurity in a child that can last a lifetime. I am saddened by how many adults have told me that their parents almost rarely gave hugs or frequently touched them in any way. In addition, for adults rarely touched as children, some will crave touch in unhealthy ways while others are negatively impacted in marriage by either avoiding physical affection or struggling to be sexually intimate with their spouse. Certainly, you don't want that for your child.

Be creative in expressing *unconditional physical love*. Freely offer pats on the back, hugs, kisses on the cheek and forehead, tousling hair, high fives, gentle arm squeezes, etc. Through touch, your child actually becomes emotionally healthy. Many studies have also found numerous physical benefits from touch. For example, blood pressure is lowered when two people touch each other. Continual physical affection with your child will also be like cement for your parent-child relationship.

Many years ago, I counseled a thirteen-year-old boy who had issues with defiance, shoplifting, vandalism, along with other problems. Brief background: The parents were divorced and their fifteen and thirteen-year-old sons were living with their mom in another state. Both boys were out of control with the law and the fifteen-year-old had recently begun snorting cocaine.

The mom decided to allow the dad to have custody of their thirteen-year-old son hoping he could "save" their son. The thirteen-year-old arrived on the first Friday of June. Two days later on Sunday, the son stole a bicycle in the neighborhood. The dad contacted me Monday morning asking for a counseling session for his son.

I met with the dad and son and spent most of the first session with the dad in private. I asked the dad to go for a walk around the block every night after dinner and intentionally touch his son a minimum of twelve times. I also asked him to implement other *Simple Habits* that are found in this Chapter Two regarding "building a strong relationship." The entire summer dad walked nightly with his son and always touched him at least twelve times.

I continued counseling them until the beginning of school. I shared with the dad many of the *Simple Habits* found in this book, particularly the lessons found in Chapters Two and Three. I am happy to report this thirteen-year-old young man became a fairly responsible teenager, good student, and their dad-son relationship became really strong.

I am not suggesting touch is the magical cure that "fixes" a child, but physical affection is significant for every person as well as a parent-child relationship. Certainly, the cliche' is true, "A touch is worth a thousand words." Perhaps set a goal for five to ten physical touches every day with your child. Consistent physical affection that happens throughout the day will be a dynamic way to ***physically love your child unconditionally***.

16. Both Quantity and Quality Time with Your Child

A parent can speak the words, "I love you," which takes a second. A parent can touch a child a dozen times per day which takes maybe fifteen seconds. Although loving words and healthy touches are essential, without also ***spending time*** with your child, those may be somewhat empty. The Bible reinforces that essential, "Making the very most of your time [on earth, recognizing and taking advantage of each opportunity and using it with wisdom and diligence]" (Ephesians 5:16 AMP).

A great synonym for love is time! When you spend time with your child you create a feeling in his or her heart of true importance and special value.

Keeping balance in life, setting priorities, and planning time for all your activities, including time with your child, is difficult for every parent. When you assess how you spend your time, then you fully understand what you truly value in life. It takes scheduling to spend time connecting with your child.

Evaluate some of your weekly activities by asking key questions:

- How much time do I spend watching television?
- How much time do I spend checking my phone or reading through the news on the internet?
- How much time do I spend with my hobbies?
- How much time do I spend on social media?
- How much time am I willing to spend with my child each day and every week?
- How much time do I spend in eye-to-eye conversation with my child each day?

I do not want you to feel guilty, but understand how scheduling significant time with your child is important.

Many parents often use most of their free time in ways which gratify their own relaxation wants. However, a parent's pleasurable activities like hobbies, reading a book, watching television, going out with friends, etc. should not be priorities ahead of spending time with the child. An *Effective Parent* also takes time to attend as many of the child's activities as possible and volunteers when opportunities arise. Please remember that one day you will have an empty nest and plenty of time for your enjoyable activities.

What may mean the most to your child is when you are busy, and you take time from your valuable schedule to be involved in his or her life, thus, making a wonderful connection. Spending just ten consecutive minutes in eye-to-eye contact with lighthearted conversation will be treasured by your child. When you make yourself available for focused quality time, your child truly knows you care.

Some parents have told me, "What is important is the quality not the quantity of time with my child." My response: "If I took an excellent quality shower one week ago but I have not bathed again over the last seven days, how bad would I smell from body odor?" Quickly, the parent realizes that it is both ***quality and quantity of time*** that truly matters. Don't make time a contest between quality and quantity! That is *either-or thinking*, which is not wholesome. Instead, think *both-and* with time, which is the positive way to activate your child's heart and is tremendously important.

Bottom line, to be an *Effective Parent* takes both *quality and quantity of time* with your child! Nothing influences your child's heart to become a responsible decision-maker like quantity and quality time together.

17. Daily Appreciation Vitamin

Saying thank-you is gratitude for something said or done. There is a difference between *gratitude* and *appreciation*. Appreciation expresses deep admiration which enhances your child's self-worth. Powerful praise is synonymous with a genuine compliment. Verbal appreciation may be the most compelling motivator for your child. Proverbs 12:25 affirms, "And how good and delightful is a word spoken at the right moment—how good it is!" (AMP).

Vitamins provide essential nutrients that you might miss in your day-to-day diet. They help improve all your biological functions from thinking to improving your health. I like to refer to praise as an *Appreciation Vitamin*. Appreciation Vitamins strengthen your child's emotional immune system to protect him or her against "infections" from life stressors.

Appreciation Vitamins must be given to your child daily to guard his or her self-worth and empower him or her to cope with life challenges.

At least once a day, please tell your child, "*I appreciate* . . ." Here are some example statements of *Appreciation Vitamins*:

- "*I appreciate* your responsible choices."
- "*I appreciate* that you are determined."
- "*I appreciate* your positive attitude."
- "*I appreciate* how hard you work."

- "*I appreciate* your outstanding character qualities."

How would you feel if someone gave you those *Appreciation Vitamins* every day? I know your answer: "Unbelievably marvelous!" You want your child to experience that same feeling. Every so often it is also beneficial to write your child a note of praise!

Please be careful when praising one child with an *Appreciation Vitamin* in front of another child. It is usually best to praise your children independently when your other children are not within earshot.

For example, if your son Scott struggles academically for various reasons, while your daughter Sue earns good grades in school, telling Sue in front of Scott, "I appreciate the great grades you earned this week," would devastate Scott's self-worth and self-confidence. Scott may have questions in his mind like, "Do my mom and dad believe in me? Are my mom and dad proud of me?"

Your children need to know that you unconditionally love both of them. When you have more than one child, positive praise is best given privately.

Your tone and body language will indicate your attitude that is manifested toward your child. A soft, loving voice and facial expression will cause your child to believe your comments are genuine. If your volume is loud, coupled with an upset demeanor, that will be devaluing to your child.

Another huge mistake some parents make is overpraise. Never inflate your child's self-esteem by overpraising your child for simple things that he or she does. When a parent frequently gives overpraise, that often creates self-centeredness, arrogance, and a false security within a child. Your praise or *Appreciation Vitamin* needs to be authentic!

Parents who are negative usually lack confidence in their own personal abilities, so they give few Appreciation Vitamins. Unfortunately, when a parent has a lack of self-worth and low self-confidence, he or she tends to possess a condemning spirit that causes him or her to be critical of others including their child. Constant criticism creates discouragement in a child while encouragement through complimentary praise instills responsibility and confidence. If you did not receive many Appreciation Vitamins as a child, you may need to practice, practice, practice giving your child Appreciation Vitamins so that it becomes a normal and natural habit for you.

I hope you now believe in the nutritional value of an *Appreciation Vitamin* for your child. *Appreciation Vitamins* are essential for your child's emotional and mental well-being. An *Effective Parent* can never give too much sincere praise!

18. Mealtimes Make A Marvelous Difference

The most underrated and least talked about parenting essential is family mealtimes at the table. In my opinion, parent-child mealtimes together are probably one of the most significant influential parenting habits because eating together makes a tremendous impact on your child in so many ways. Please realize mealtimes are for enjoyment, modeling manners, at times lovingly encouraging eating etiquette, and not continually correcting your child.

When a child is struggling behaviorally or academically, I have found most of the time meals are not eaten together as a family. I hear reports that each family member eats nearly every meal in a different part of the house--bedroom, living room in front of the television, the basement, BUT not together. When everyone starts eating together and applying the following 10 goals, I have amazingly witnessed positive family life improvement, as well as a child's behavior becoming more responsible.

Shown below are 10 goals of having mealtimes together as a family:

1. ***Before and after meal prayers***. Christian families live their faith throughout the day every day in so many ways.

When you have before and after meal prayers, it emphasizes Almighty God is the foundation of your home.

2. ***Spending quality time together***. One of the best synonyms for ***love*** is ***time***. When all family members eat at the table, they are demonstrating love through time together rather than eating in front of the television, computer, in the bedroom, etc. Think about it, each week, if you are able to have nine family meals that are even twenty minutes in length, that provides three hours of family connecting time.
3. ***Meaningful eye contact***. The eyes are "windows to the heart." Having a close physical proximity with bonding eye contact provides a wonderful opportunity to show warmth, care, and love.
4. ***Table manners are both learned and taught***. "Please," "thank you," and "you are welcome" are courtesies that healthy people demonstrate regularly. Mealtimes together provide those opportunities for good manners. For example, "Will you please pass the mashed potatoes?" "Thank you." "You are welcome." In addition, politeness is often missing in troubled families, and mealtimes together allow politeness to permeate the family atmosphere.
5. ***Develop responsible behaviors by setting and clearing the table***. A strong work ethic is one foundational goal for healthy self-esteem. Having children both set the table and then clear the dishes is a very basic way to develop a responsible work ethic.
6. ***Opportunity for a daily compliment***. Every person loves to be complimented, especially children. Mark Twain said he can live two weeks on one good compliment. You can easily give your child an *Appreciation Vitamin* about almost anything, like praising your child for setting the table or removing the dishes with an "*I appreciate*."
7. ***Develop a positive attitude***. There should be absolutely no "problem-talk" during meals. When all family members

avoid discussing problems about home repairs, school difficulties, work issues, etc., that allows for a stress-free time for simply enjoying one another's company and being positive.

8. ***Values are learned through mealtime discussions.*** Some studies suggest children learn more values during family meals than in church and school. Through mealtimes, help your child develop Biblical values through your discussions.
9. ***Ask valuable questions.*** Einstein's mother used to ask him when he came home from school, "Did you ask any good questions today?" Parents can ask that question and other important questions like, "What were two good things that happened today?" or "Will you please tell me the most exciting thing that happened today?" or "What was something you learned at school today?" or "What kindness did you express toward someone today?" etc. Valuable questions also help create optimism and a positive attitude within your child.
10. ***Stewardship of God's blessings.*** Teaching children to eat all the food on their plate reinforces the principles of stewardship. Help your child overcome waste because that is a problem in so many areas of society. Throwing away food leads to the false belief that waste is acceptable and good stewardship of God's blessings is not important. When selecting food and drink portions, children need to choose an appropriate amount. Of course, a child can always have additional helpings. Please note that continually leaving food on a plate may at times be a sign for an eating disorder demonstrated by restricting the intake of food.

Many parent books often suggest a regular *family meeting*. When families have almost all meals together that automatically provides an opportunity for a family meeting after the meal is finished for discussing any parent-child matters. However, it is usually best for these conversations to not happen more than once a week.

There are probably more valuable lessons your child learns when you eat almost every meal with each other at the table. As often as possible, eat together as a family and make your meal-times relaxing, enjoyable experiences for every family member.

19. Positive Labels Are Essential

Your child will fulfill whatever positive or negative labels are regularly imprinted on his or her mind. With high probability, your child will live up to the reputation he or she is given on an ongoing basis. Labels often shape your child's present life and even his or her entire adult life.

If you harmfully give your child negative labels, the probabilities are high your child will become what you repeatedly told him or her. Examples of negative statements:

- "You are argumentative"
- "You are bossy"
- "You are helpless"
- "You are obnoxious"
- "You are lazy"

Your child will start believing that is one of his or her personality traits, which is a serious problem.

On the positive side, when you tell your child, "You are hard-working," your child will probably have a wonderful work ethic. When you tell your child, he or she has a positive attitude, your child will probably have an optimistic outlook on life. When you tell your child, he or she is very determined, with high probability he or she will possess a "Never Give Up" spirit.

Years ago, a mom brought her six-year-old daughter to counseling because she was "extremely shy." With her daughter by her side she said, "My husband and I are very concerned about our daughter because she is so very shy around others." I asked the six-year-old a few questions and she responded fairly well. My first comment to the girl was, "I appreciate how well you talked when answering my questions. May I call you 'Miss Talker'?" She smiled and said "Yes."

Then, I met with mom in private. I suggested that the mom and dad, along with her teacher, catch the six-year-old talking and give the six-year-old a positive label with the statement, "I appreciate how well you are *talking*." I also asked the mom, dad, and the teacher to never use the word "shy" or any other negative labels with their daughter.

Whenever mom brought the six-year-old to counseling, I always called the girl "Miss Talker" throughout the session. Thankfully, mom, dad, and the teacher all gave the sweet six-year-old the "Talker" label, as well. After approximately six months, what did the girl become? You are right, a "Talker."

Coincidentally, in September of that same year, a mom brought her seven-year-old son for counseling because he was "mean." In front of her son, the mom told me, "Our son is unbearably mean at home with us, his siblings, and the teacher no longer wants him in her classroom because of his "meanness." The young man was sitting nicely on my sofa so I asked him if I may call him "Mr. Nice." Like the sweet girl he smiled and said, "Yes."

I gave this mom, dad, and teacher the same suggestion for this young man. I asked all three to catch him being *nice* and then say, "I appreciate how *nice* you are acting toward others." What did this young man become? You are right, "Mr. Nice."

In February, when I met with this "nice" young man I asked him, "How long are you going to be 'Mr. Nice'?" I was surprised when he said, "Dr. Schroeder, 200 more days." Kids certainly make unbelievable statements at times. His comment brought a big smile to my face and I asked him to walk over to me and, with my finger, I wrote the word "nice" on his forehead. Then, I told him, "You are now going to be 'nice' until the day you go to heaven." Thankfully, this seven-year-old continued to be "Mr. Nice."

A final example is a thirty-five-year-old dad who was a chief executive officer of a major corporation. I met with this man and his wife without the children and thoroughly explained the tremendous impact of ***labels***. With a sad heart, the dad shared that he had been giving his children negative labels like "lazy," "disorganized," "loser," etc. and his children were fulfilling those negative labels. Unintentionally, he and his wife were hurting all three kids' self-image as well as destructively shaping behavior.

Surprisingly, the CEO said, throughout his childhood, his dad told him thousands of times, "You are a leader," which was the exact position he held in his corporation at a young age. That same day, he and his wife started ***positive labeling*** their children and almost immediately their children began to become more responsible decision-makers.

I encourage you to identify two deficits in each of your children. Then, identify a *positive label* to counter each deficit. Without specific positives to look for, you will have a difficult time sending your child positive messages to overcome deficits. For example, the opposite of obnoxious is *kind*; the opposite of lazy is *hardworking*; the counter to defiant is *cooperative*; and a simple one, the opposite of disrespectful is *respectful*. When both parents *catch* their child doing something right and give *positive labels*, the child will begin living up to that reputation.

One caution, do not use flattery or be insincere when giving your positive labels. Your child will see through your untruthfulness and your positive labeling will actually backfire. Always be a "Goodfinder" with your child, especially when it comes to giving *positive labels*.

Keep in mind that a child with special needs, whether physical or mental, needs to receive unconditional love, praise, and positive labels, as well. The positive labels may be, "I am blessed to be your parent," "You are so special," "You are a wonderful child of God," and "You have a beautiful kind heart."

20. Regular One-on-One Activities

Every child loves one-on-one time with each of his or her parents. Ask yourself a key question: "How much one-on-one time do I have with my child—just the two of us?"

Some families are like a school of fish where they do everything together day-in-day-out. One or both parents simply refuse to understand the importance of one-on-one activities, which ends up being detrimental to their child. One-on-one bonding time just does not happen by accident.

Plan to spend time alone with each of your children both indoors and outdoors. Play mentally stimulating games like checkers, chess, monopoly, dominoes, and other fun board games. Together, go putt on a practice green, ride bikes, enjoy a video game together, play catch with a baseball, build a fort in your living room, shoot baskets, watch a television show together while giving physical touches, etc. Do whatever it takes to spend time alone with each of your children.

One of the best benefits of one-on-one activities is the wonderful opportunity to give your child compliments and praise with an *Appreciation Vitamin*. For example, if you play catch with your child for fifty throws, that provides an opportunity for fifty comments like, "Great throw!" "Very nice form!" "Terrific catching!" "Wonderful accuracy!" "Fantastic job!" Playing a video game with your child for an hour would also afford numerous opportunities for you to compliment and praise your child. Plan and be creative with your *one-on-one activities*.

21. Monthly Date Your Child

Of all the suggestions in this book, none may be more valuable than this *monthly date-your-child* lesson. I have had hundreds of parents tell me that this lesson is what made a significant positive difference in their parent-child relationship.

A date is approximately forty-five to sixty minutes *outside the home.* An ideal date is eating with your child because you can sit across from each other for an excellent eye-to-eye heart talk. Within the family budget, always permit your child to select the date. When your child chooses the date, he or she will feel extra special and more relaxed because it was his or her decision.

A *monthly date-your-child* does not have to be expensive. Perhaps go for an ice cream cone or a shake. Maybe eat at a fast-food restaurant that your child enjoys. Without interrogating, the goal is to attentively look in your child's eyes and ask "How" and "What" questions to learn more about his or her thoughts, feelings, fears, dreams, etc. Hundreds of parents have told me that it is unbelievable how their children open up about their inner world more outside the home over food than ever inside the home.

Let your child lead the discussion and don't push him or her to discuss major concerns unless the child brings it up. Also, as a parent driving to the date, during the date, and on the way back home, absolutely never discuss any concerns you might have for your child or problems in his or her life! The goal is for your child to look forward to these *monthly dates* with you as his or her parent.

Married couples with two children may consider having their *monthly date your child* on a weeknight to replace dinner at home. For example, one Wednesday night mom takes one child and dad the other child. Two weeks later, the parents switch children and once again go out for dinner.

Years ago, I counseled with a fifteen-year-old young man and his dad experiencing a bad father-son relationship. When the dad and son attended the first session, the son told his dad he would sit on the sofa alone and his dad would have to sit in the chair. Toward the end of that session, I asked the son if he would go for lunch with his dad on Saturday. I remember distinctly the son saying to me, "Dr. Schroeder, did you hear what I've been telling you the entire session? I don't like my dad and want nothing to do with him."

I worked hard to discover the teenager's two favorite restaurants. I convinced the teenager to go for a Saturday lunch with his dad and the teen selected an Italian restaurant. Then, I looked the dad in the eyes and asked, "Will you please absolutely not criticize, complain, correct, or condemn your son on the drive to the restaurant, during the meal, and on the way home?" The dad agreed and I asked him to tell his son, "I promise to avoid the Cs of criticism, correction, complaints, and condemnation."

The son ordered spaghetti with meat balls at the Italian restaurant. Half-way through the meal, the fifteen-year-old son put down his fork, grabbed a handful of spaghetti with a meatball, and stuffed it in his mouth. He continued to finish his lunch using his hand instead of his fork.

The dad could hear my voice echoing in his ears, "Avoid criticizing, complaining, correcting, or condemning." The dad and son had a pleasant conversation throughout the meal and on the drive home. I truly admire the dad's self-restraint because he said nothing about his son's poor manners on Saturday afternoon, as well as all day Sunday and Monday. After coming home from work on Tuesday evening, the dad asked his son, "If you pick that Italian restaurant for our monthly date will you please use a fork next time?" The teenager gave a big smile and said, "Sure, dad."

Starting that Tuesday evening, they had a fresh start for what would become a wonderful father-son relationship. Certainly, the mom and dad used many of the *Simple Habits* in this book, but it's the *monthly date-your-child* that began to restore the dad's broken relationship with his son.

I counseled another dad who had a terrible relationship with his four children. This dad began monthly dating each child and shared that his four children always picked the same Mexican restaurant for Saturday lunch. After eating at the same restaurant fifty-two Saturdays a year, the dad shared, "I have eaten every appetizer, entrée, and dessert on that menu. Every Friday I beg for a change of restaurants. Please help me."

Dad was only teasing me because he loved self-sacrificing his food interests and thoroughly enjoyed meeting the culinary delights for each child even if it was the same restaurant. Like the dad of the fifteen-year-old son, this dad eventually experienced a more solid relationship with his children.

In both these examples, the moms already had good relationships with their children. Nonetheless, the moms also had gratifying monthly dates with each of their children.

I honestly believe *monthly date-your-child* will become a fun and valuable aspect for your parent-child relationship. Begin planning one-on-one time today and thoroughly relish the opportunity to attentively listen and nurture your child.

22. Weekly Family Nights

The time you spend at home together with your family is important because that positively impacts your child. Being physically present with your family on a weekly basis is a major parenting goal. Of course, you realize that "weekly" is an ideal goal that may not always be achievable.

I suggest ***weekly family nights*** occur on non-school nights, meaning Friday, Saturday, or Sunday nights when everyone is less stressed. The goal is a relaxed, pleasurable evening together without any problem discussion. Provide your child with many options like movies, board games, card games, etc. Kids and adults love to eat junk food. Consider allowing your weekly family nights to be comfort food meals with your child selecting the pizza or fast-food place.

Allow your child to make the family night meal and activity selections. If you have more than one child, alternate having each child pick dinner and the evening entertainment. Having your child make the selection will also more likely encourage his or her involvement.

Conversational interactions within a family are foundational for building stronger relationships. Learning to effectively communicate will make a significant difference for your child as an adult. *Weekly family nights* are significant in accomplishing that parenting objective.

23. Make Memorable Experiences

Memorable Experiences are any fun activity outside your home where your child will fondly look back on the experience. Certainly, Lessons 20, 21, and 22 could turn out to be some of those wonderful ***memorable experiences*** for your child.

When it comes to making *memorable experiences,* the possibilities are endless. Depending on where you live, visit the zoo, go to a children's museum, attend a baseball, basketball or football game, or some other local attraction. At your house, sleep in a tent outside. If affordable, you might take mini-vacations or one-week vacations to a special location each year.

For Halloween, take your child to a local farm to go through a maze and find a pumpkin to carve. Perhaps establish a tradition to find a live Christmas tree together and visit Santa Claus. If available, go on a Polar Express train with your child. At Easter, hide eggs and visit the Easter Bunny.

With your child, make a written list of fun activities that he or she wants to do as a family. With your child's list of pleasurable pursuits, do whatever you can to accomplish those endeavors. Be intentional with achieving your child's written list of ***memorable experiences***.

CHAPTER 3

HABITS THAT HELP APPLY THE RULES

Effectively applying rules is loving discipline that leads and guides a child toward adulthood. The Latin word *disciplina* means instruction. When any form of discipline is necessary, the goal is to teach or train your child, not to hurt or punish him or her. Proverbs 19:18 declares, "Discipline your children, for in that there is hope" (NIV).

Eli's sons were immoral, disrespectful, and unruly (1 Samuel). God was angry that Eli did not fulfill his responsibilities as a father by correcting his sons' bad behavior. From this sad story, we learn Almighty God wants parents to administer loving, fair, and consistent discipline for their children's sake.

All children misbehave and make mistakes, so the goal is to provide loving discipline. This chapter speaks volumes about the importance of effectively applying rules, so your child learns to accept responsibility for his or her behavior. As a parent, you want your child to understand that his or her decisions result in either positive rewards or negative consequences.

An *Effective Parent* strives for *obedience* to instill moral Biblical values, self-discipline, and conscientious choices within the child. All these *Simple Habits* are important, but the lessons in

Chapter Two, *Build a Strong Relationship*, and this chapter, *Apply the Rules*, are essential parenting skills for leading your child to one day function as a responsible, reliable adult.

24. Establish Rules

Through Moses, God gave the Ten Commandments as guiding principles for life. The Sermon on the Mount (Matthew 5-7) also focuses on what it means to be a disciple of Christ. The Sermon on the Mount set forth golden rules for all people to live by, including your child.

Rules are everywhere in society, the workplace, school, and yes, even present in the home. Rules provide limits, but at the same time, guarantee freedom because acceptable behavior is defined. Rules create order in your child's life producing a relaxed home environment. When your child learns to obey rules within your home, he or she is also likely to obey rules of society.

Without rules, your child lives in uncertainty and has a persistent insecure feeling of being directionless in life. Without boundaries, your child will lack self-discipline and self-confidence. Without rules, your child will not learn from his or her mistakes. Without limits, your home will be a place of constant stress and tension. Without rules, your child will not understand your desire for him or her to be a responsible, reliable individual.

Of course, your child will challenge your rules as well as question your ability to enforce the rules. Adam and Eve hid from God and lied to Him. When your child misbehaves, do not be offended or take it personally because your child is human, and it is normal for every child to make mistakes.

An excellent synonym for a *rule* is *expectation*. Your child wants to understand what to expect from you, so he or she knows how to behave based upon your rules that organize his or her life. Your child wants to know that your rules are consistent and not temporary ideas. Shown below are seven guidelines for establishing beneficial rules for your child.

1. Specifically define your rules rather than share vague expectations. For example, "Play nicely in the house" is not as precise as, "Use your inside voice," "Don't jump on the furniture," "Don't throw balls in the house," etc.
2. If necessary, explain the rule and perhaps the purpose for the rule.
3. Some rules are firm while others are flexible. A firm rule for safety would be a five-year old having the expectation to not leave the front yard. On nonschool days, an eight-year-old may have a time limit for video games. However, on a nonschool day, after playing outside for seven hours, a parent may have the flexibility to allow an extra amount of time that day to enjoy video games.
4. Many rules change over time as your child ages. Per the example in number 3, a fifteen-year-old will not be confined to the front yard.
5. Rules should be ***reasonable*** because the goal is to benefit your child with expectations, so he or she grows toward adulthood. Oppressive, harsh rules will crush your child's spirit and harm your parent-child relationship. For example, I counseled a family that thought a 3-hour timeout was appropriate for their eight-year-old son. This eight-year-old boy was anxious, depressed, and broken emotionally.
6. Remember your body language, facial expression, and tone of voice are essential when conveying an expectation or rule.
7. You will learn how to clearly state an expectation or rule in Lessons 28, 29, and 30.

Rules are essential for your home as well as society. Setting household rules conveys love for your child and trains your child to eventually practice self-discipline.

25. Logical and Natural Consequences

Logical consequences are connected to the problem behavior in order to produce a positive impact on a child's future decision-making. *Natural consequences* are "penalties" that happen normally because of poor decisions without a parent even needing to intervene.

Logical consequences are those disciplinary actions that are given by you as a parent. When a child experiences logical consequences for breaking the rules, he or she learns powerful lessons about making correct choices. Logical consequences are often easily accepted by children when those consequences are reasonable and always given in a firm, kind manner.

Some examples of logical consequences are:

- Going to time-out for being disrespectful
- After being late for curfew Friday night, not going out on Saturday night
- After misbehaving at school not having technology that same night
- Removal of toys for a period of time for not putting those toys away
- Eliminating time with friends for not completing chores

When your child makes an unhealthy decision or breaks the rules, try to connect logical consequences with the misbehavior as much as possible. Your goals are to teach dependable behavior and responsible choices with your consequences, not to hurt your child in anyway.

Logical consequences should be brief, and the amount of time should match the offense. For an elementary age child maybe the length of time for losing a privilege is thirty minutes. You can easily double or even triple the time if your child does not immediately correct his or her behavior. Usually after doubling the time your child will choose the right action to end the consequence.

Examples of being brief and how to use time effectively with your logical consequences will be described more in Lesson 26.

Natural consequences are those actions that happen without your parental intervention. Natural consequences are wonderful life experiences because they directly impact your child for what he or she chose to do or not do.

Examples of natural consequences are:

A teenager goes to the lake with friends and out of carelessness loses a cell phone in the water. Now the teen understands the value of money having to work in order to purchase another cell phone.

A junior high school youngster misbehaves in class and the principal sends him straight home after school, thus, missing his favorite extracurricular activity of robotics.

Against a parent's instruction, a young child is playing with his or her glass piggybank, drops it, so now the child does not have a piggy bank until he or she saves enough allowance money to buy one.

A teenager stays up too late, is very tired the next day at school, and experiences a difficult time focusing on schoolwork.

A parent asks a child to place the lunch sack in his or her backpack. The child forgets to carry out the request. Either the child goes hungry that day or he or she has to talk with the teacher about a lunch for that day and request a bill be sent to mom and dad.

Natural consequences are not appropriate if they have the potential to hurt your child in adult life. Three good examples of harmful future consequences are brushing teeth, grades, and reckless driving. If a child rarely or never brushed teeth, tooth decay would be a major problem. If a child decided not to do any schoolwork, a parent would not say, "One day you will not have the grades to go to college," rather, a parent would intervene with logical consequences. Finally, if a teen was continually speeding or driving recklessly, a parent certainly would not say, "You keep driving this way and you will kill yourself or someone else."

Natural consequences are not appropriate if a child is a danger to himself/herself or another child. For example, if a young child was playing in the street, a parent definitely would not say, "You better play in the yard otherwise you might get hit by a car." Or if a child was swinging a stick around another child, he or she may accidentally poke that child in the eye. Immediately, a parent would put an end to that dangerous situation.

As with all consequences, please remember to exhibit compassion, calmness, and support for what your child is learning. Consequences are excellent motivators for your child to correct his or her behavior and make more positive decisions in the future. Society and the workplace function through consequences, so begin as a parent to lead your child through consequences as well.

26. Consequences, Taking Away Privileges, or Onerous Chores

Galatians 6:7-8 states, "A man reaps what he sows. Whoever sows to please their flesh, from the flesh will reap destruction; whoever sows to please the Spirit, from the Spirit will reap eternal life." In a similar way, parents can implement the sow-reap principle to help a child understand this norm is part of daily life. Your child benefits from understanding that good choices create a pleasant life while poor choices lead to unhappiness.

Probably the best way to help your child become a responsible decision-maker is through giving ***consequences, taking away the child's privileges,*** or disciplining the child with ***onerous chores.*** Through your facial expression, tone of voice, and words you absolutely want your child to understand you are not upset with him or her. The goal for all three is to help your child:

- Know he or she misbehaved.
- Learn from that mistake.
- Experience unpleasantness from one of these three applications producing an impactful reminder not to commit that misconduct again.

Always think, "Will this discipline application help my child make a better decision next time?"

Make sure to keep the consequences or loss of privileges brief, because lengthy consequences will break your child's spirit. However, for recurring misbehavior, you can always lengthen the time. I realize it is also difficult to define "brief." For example, a five-year old child being disrespectful would go to time-out for a brief five minutes. Or a teenager with missed homework assignments may lose technology privileges for one evening.

Almost every teenager will make a poor choice and be late for curfew. Some parents may initially think, "You decided to be grounded the *next five years of your life* because of missing curfew." Certainly, that is a light-hearted comment, and no *Effective Parent* would apply that consequence.

If a teen is late for a weekend curfew, a brief, appropriate consequence would be to not go out the next weekend night. In the next couple of months, if the teen was once again late for a weekend curfew, the consequence could be doubled to two weekend nights. For example, the teen is late for curfew on a Friday night, two weekend nights would be Saturday night and the following Friday night.

I counseled with parents and their teenage son who was an outstanding high school athlete. The parents had been giving lengthy consequences when their son made poor decisions and he was continually angry and disrespectful. For example, if their son was disrespectful even one time, his parents would not let him leave home for the weekend. I stressed that both parents really needed to shorten their consequences.

At the next counseling session, the dad reported that the son was disrespectful on Saturday around 5:00 p.m. The dad said to his son, "*Either* act respectful *or* you will have to wait for one hour to go out to eat with your friends, *you decide*." Disrespect continued, so the one-hour consequence was given. The dad said a second time, "*Either* act respectful *or* you will have to wait for two hours to go out to eat with your friends, *you decide*." The son continued being disrespectful, so the dad doubled the consequence with, "*You now decided* to wait for two hours before going out with your friends." With that two-hour consequence, the son walked away and was no longer disrespectful. I can happily share that the teenager's parents continued to use brief consequences and their relationship with their son significantly improved, as well as his respect.

I met with an elementary school principal and his wife who were having major problems with their children. Unfortunately, the principal and his wife had been breaking the spirits of their children through lengthy consequences. With both parents, I stressed brief consequences not lengthy ones. The principal sadly commented he was parenting just like he did when he was a first-year teacher. He was so very frustrated with himself because he was asking his teaching staff to apply brief consequences at school, but he and his wife were doing the opposite with their children.

The principal went on to explain that, as a first-year teacher, he would discipline a disruptive student with lengthy consequences, which proved ineffective:

"I would tell the student, 'Either work quietly or you will miss recess the remainder of this week, you decide.' Of course, that was not a brief consequence. Then, when the student continued to disrupt the learning environment, I would say, 'You decided to miss recess the remainder of this week because you misbehaved.' The next day, when the troublesome student started acting up again, I was out of ammunition because all I could use as a consequence was the following week of recesses. My first-year teaching was rough until I learned to use just one recess at a time, a brief consequence."

The principal and his wife started utilizing brief consequences with their children and family life dramatically changed for the positive.

However, when your child makes a major wrong decision, then lengthy consequences are totally necessary. For example, a girl who was a junior in high school consumed too much alcohol and drove home drunk on a Friday night. Certainly, she could have killed herself or another person while driving inebriated which was a decision with life and death consequences.

In counseling, I suggested to the parents that they consider not allowing their daughter to go out for one month because of the seriousness of the situation. They agreed and implemented my suggested lengthy consequence. If you can believe it, the first weekend night of freedom, their daughter got drunk once again and drove herself home. This time the parents doubled the consequence by not allowing their daughter to go out for two months.

On a monthly basis, I continued counseling with the parents and their daughter until she graduated from high school. The parents were not absolutely certain if she learned to be a better decision-maker with alcohol. However, the parents reported that they never smelled alcohol on their daughter's breath again throughout her high school years.

Please understand that serious wrong decisions may require ***lengthy consequences*** while mundane misbehavior leads to brief, minor ones that can easily be doubled or even tripled. In addition, ***taking away privileges*** is based on the same brief standard.

A third way to deal with objectionable behavior is through onerous chores. Examples of onerous chores are: scrubbing the bathroom tub, pulling weeds in the flower bed, cleaning all the toilets in the house, scrubbing the kitchen floor or bathroom floor, dusting furniture throughout the entire house, etc. The goal of onerous chores is to teach your child to adopt better decision-making skills.

Every decision made by your child has either a positive or negative outcome. ***Consequences, taking away the child's privileges*** or disciplining him or her with ***onerous chores*** will assist you in decreasing your child's poor choices in order to increase positive decisions and outcomes.

27. Discipline the First Time Decisively and Consistently

A major problem for many parents is not providing ***first time*** discipline by ineffectively continuing to give numerous chances for their child to be obedient. A child's future decision-making is actually hurt when the parent is not swift, definitive, and dependable with discipline. A parent who is not a first-time disciplinarian, experiences frustration, is usually pushed to his or her anger limit, and unfortunately, frequently responds randomly which is harmful for the child. An *Effective Parent* needs to follow Matthew 5:37, "But let your statement be, 'Yes, yes' or 'No, no' [a firm yes or no]" (AMP).

Every experienced, successful teacher starts immediately, the very first day, with rules and firm discipline! A seasoned teacher does not say, "The first week will be a lot of fun. I will start with a few rules and, when they don't obey the rules, I will give my students three, four, five, or even ten warnings." Experienced teachers know that kind of approach leads to a chaotic environment and a long, miserable school year.

A veteran teacher has the philosophy, "The first day I will explain the rules, decisively apply the rules the ***first time***, and thus, establish a wonderful learning environment for the entire school year." Ninety-eight percent of students in that classroom will respect and admire that effective teacher. As a parent, have the same philosophy as every competent teacher to have a loving environment for your child's eighteen years at home. Likewise, as a parent, explain the rules so there is a clear understanding of what is expected, as well as why the child should not do something.

The earlier in life your child begins having major difficulties at home or school, the greater likelihood your child may seriously struggle through his or her teen years and even adult life. Sadly, too many parents believe they do not need to take discipline seriously until a child is four or five years old. That is simply an unwholesome idea. During the first five years, some parents will even laugh or smile in front of their child at mischievous behavior. I have observed parents chuckling when their child disobediently walked out of a Sunday school classroom or grinned when their child screamed about a rule. Effectively parenting a child during the first five years is essential, don't wait!

In terms of learning respect and obedience, ages five to twelve are extremely important. If your child is not seriously disrespectful or has few behavioral difficulties during the first twelve years, your child will probably not have significant issues as a teenager and adult. Absolutely ***discipline the first time*** by starting at approximately two years of age.

The key to effective discipline is to follow through on your first request for obedience. Regrettably, some parenting books suggest that a parent count to three or at least give several warnings before acting. It is simply illogical to keep moving the boundary over and over again. A child eventually learns how many warnings the parent will give before enforcing the rule. When a parent continually caves on the limits, he or she also rewards and reinforces a child's ongoing misbehavior. A child given an instruction or a "Will you please" (Lesson 28) needs to either *obediently* respond the first time or suffer an immediate consequence.

When parents tell me in counseling, "My child won't listen" or "Nothing seems to work with my child," they are implying, "I don't know how to enforce the rules," by *disciplining the first time decisively and consistently*. If you are repeatedly saying your child's name or requesting obedience two, three, four, or more times, you are not only enabling your child to be disobedient and irresponsible, but you are creating a defiant child. When that happens with a child under thirteen, the teen and adult years can often be extremely troublesome.

In summary, give your child an opportunity to fulfill your ***request one time***. Do not keep moving the boundary! Loving your child requires that you avoid second chances and not give numerous warnings, but demonstrate your leadership by developing the habit of positively responding the *first time*. When your child misbehaves or makes a poor decision, be immediate and firm in correcting that child with a consequence in order to ***discipline the first time decisively and consistently***.

28. Ask Politely: Will You Please. . .

Our Heavenly Father expects us to follow principles and commands found in the Bible. Proverbs 13:1 indicates, "A wise son heeds his father's instruction; but a mocker does not listen to rebuke" (NIV). Thus, expect your child to follow your instructions and guidance. One step to providing a decision-making opportunity is to offer a choice in the form of a question.

Every person, even a child, wants the freedom to be in charge of his or her life. Whenever a request or instruction is made, it is best to politely ***ask*** the question, "***Will you please***?" A sentence comes across as a demand, command, or order which often creates rebellion. Use "***Will***" because that word is softer on the ears than "would," "could," or "can." There are times a sentence instruction is appropriate, but most of the time ***ask politely*** the question, "***Will you please***?"

An example of a commanding sentence is, "Please be respectful," which provides no opportunity for your child to decide. As a parent, you are telling your child what to do rather than seeking obedience. Again, sentences are the exception not the rule.

"*Will you please*" also increases the likelihood for more compliance from your child because he or she is making his or her own decision rather than being told what to do. Well over a thousand parents have shared with me that "*Will you please*" not only increased obedience but also strengthened the love in their parent-child relationship.

An example of asking politely is "*Will you please* be respectful?" Your child now needs to decide to either be respectful or continue being disrespectful. "*Will you please*" indicates you are not attempting to control by ordering your child to be respectful. The "*Will you please*" requesting process, assists your child in making a respectful, mature decision to follow your parental leadership.

You want your child to treat others with respect, so model respect for your child. Use a question when asking your child to do something or when you invite him or her to help with a responsibility. An *Effective Parent* rarely uses a sentence with an instruction, but instead uses the question, "*Will you please . . .*" Watch your tone by asking "***Will you please***" with a voice that is loving, encouraging, and strong.

29. Either/Or/You Decide

Every parental teaching situation is different and there may be times you think it is best to give your child a second chance. Be a *first-time* disciplinarian, but when appropriate, have flexibility by providing a second warning with **Either/Or/You decide** and **You decided/Because/Try again.**

For example, you want your daughter Pam to share a toy with her sister Sue because Pam already played with the toy a long time. The entire sequence would be:

1. "Pam, *will you please* share your toy with Sue for fifteen minutes?"

2. If Pam refuses, say, "***Either*** share your toy with Pam ***or*** go to time-out. ***You decide***."
3. If Pam continues to misbehave firmly state, "Pam, ***you decided*** to go to time-out ***because*** you did not share and made a poor choice."
4. "You can ***try again*** to share after time-out."

Using another example, if your child were disrespectful, the correction would happen this way:

1. "*Will you please* be respectful?"
2. If disrespect continues, say, "***Either*** act respectful ***or*** go to time-out, ***you decide***."
3. If your child is still disrespectful and disobedient, your response would be, "***You decided*** to go to time-out ***because*** you are still disrespectful."
4. "You can ***try again*** to be respectful after time-out."

Learning *Either/Or/You decide* and *You decided/Because/Try again* appears so very simple, but is extremely difficult to memorize. You will probably need to practice saying those words over and over before it becomes somewhat natural.

Another important challenge is mentioning what your child did wrong after "***You decided,***" rather than giving the *consequence first* followed by reasons for the consequence. It feels normal to focus on your child's disobedience and wrong decision with "*You decided to be disrespectful*" but that is incorrect. Always mention the consequence immediately after "*You decided*" and then the reasons. Hence, the correct response is "***You decided*** to go to time-out (consequence) ***because*** you are continuing to be disrespectful (reasons)."

Due to the long "I" sound, I prefer the word "***decide***" versus the words "chose" or "choose." I think the "I" rings in your child's ear better than the "O." However, the mother of all learning is repetition so whether you use "*decide*" or "chose," both parents should always use the exact same word when giving a consequence. Speaking the precise same words is very important for your child. Repetition with the same parenting language reinforces learning and that produces responsible decisions.

After using ***Either/Or/You decide*** numerous times with their child, some parents have told me that their child will repeat back, "Either/Or/You decide, Either/Or/You decide, I am tired of having to make decisions all the time." A worthy goal as a parent is for your child to make a similar comment to you one day.

You can also use *Either/Or/You decide* to prevent *sibling rivalry*. Many parents play "judge or jury" when two children are arguing which is not only ineffective but harmful to sibling relationships. Being "judge or jury" often forces children to lie and may even place a wedge in the relationship between both children.

For example, a parent is working in the kitchen and hears a brother and sister aggressively arguing over a video game in the family room. Too many parents will go into the family room, be "judge or jury," and ask both children to share their version of what happened. Sadly, the child that lies the best will get out of trouble and be allowed to continue playing the video game. The "losing" child will be upset with the parent and his or her sibling creating family stress.

Important goals for every child are to learn self-control and negotiation skills. Both skills are so very necessary for succeeding in adult relationships. To handle the aforementioned example, an *Effective Parent* will go into the family room and say to both children, "***Either*** cooperate with each other ***or*** no video games for one hour, ***you decide***." Then, the parent should go back into the kitchen without any further discussion.

If those two kids demonstrate self-control and negotiation skills, they will continue playing video games. If the two children continue to argue, the parent would go back into the family room and say, "The two of ***you decided*** to not play video games for one hour ***because*** you are continuing to argue. You can ***try again*** later." This sibling rivalry example shows how an *Effective Parent* can remain firm, friendly, and more importantly, help both children learn a valuable lesson of self-control and negotiation skills with future relationships.

When you see with your own eyes one child harm another child, it is not necessary to use ***Either/Or/You Decide***. You truly observed the misbehavior so you can either ask, "***Will you please*** apologize and not do that again?" Or give an immediate consequence with a "***You decided/Because***."

30. When You/Then You

When you/Then you is probably in the top ten of all the *Simple Habits* in this book. *When you/Then you* is often referred to as "Grandma's Law." Grandma would say, "***When you*** eat all your vegetables and chicken, ***then you*** may have a piece of the pie I baked you." Thankfully, ***When you/Then you*** is also one of the easiest skills to implement in your parenting approach for obedient decision-making.

One of your goals is to help your child become a very responsible decision-maker, so one day, he or she will be a successful, independent adult. Dependable decision-making is achieved by giving your child choices on a regular basis with:

- *Will you please . . .*
- *Either/Or/You decide*
- *When you/Then you*

One of the best ways to provide decision-making opportunities and lessen the tension within your parent-child relationship is through *When you/Then you* choices. There are parents who use a similar but not as effective version of "When you/Then you" with the words "*IF* you/Then you." Never say "*If you/Then you*" because that indicates a lack of confidence in your child's abilities to succeed.

For example, I say to you, "*If you* read this Christian parenting book, *then you* may become an *Effective Parent*." I am really not sure that you will read the book. However, when I say, "*When you* read this Christian parenting book, *then you* may become an *Effective Parent*." I now totally believe in you, have confidence that you will read this book, and know it is just a matter of when." I hope you can understand the difference and will never say "If you/Then you" to your child, but only say "***When you/Then you.***"

It is usually best to use *When you/Then you* with chores and responsibilities. Examples are: "*When you* take out the trash, *then you* may play outside"; "*When you* put on your pajamas, *then you* may watch your television show"; "*When you* do your homework, *then you* may play computer games"; and "*When you* brush your teeth, *then you* may play with your favorite toy."

I counseled a father who was very disappointed that his fifteen-year-old daughter would not clean her bathroom even when he and his wife "yelled, threatened, or bargained." I explained the *When you/Then you* parenting tool and suggested that, when he arrived home, he use this skill with his daughter regarding the bathroom situation. I had the dad repeat three times softly and slowly, "*When you* clean your bathroom, *then you* may use your cell phone." Technology is a wonderful privilege that can influence your child to become a responsible decision-maker.

The next session, he walked in my office with a relieved, big smile and said:

"Parenting has become so much easier. I went home, asked for my daughter's cell phone, and said, '*When you* clean your bathroom, *then you* may have your cell phone.' After ten minutes, my daughter said she was finished. I checked and found a somewhat dirty sink. Again, I said '*When you* clean the sink, *then you* may have your cell phone.' Less than three minutes later, she had cleaned the sink and I gave her the cell phone."

I appreciated his wonderful use of *When you/Then you* and reminded him that "Being a parent is still challenging. However, with the correct verbal skills, there will be reduced stress in your home, and you are less drained as a parent."

Always believe in your child and have faith he or she can and will succeed at all his or her endeavors! Use ***When you/Then you*** almost daily to motivate your child to accomplish chores and responsibilities.

31. Time-Out

When a consequence is necessary, ***Time-out*** is probably the most used tool by nearly every parent. Time-out may be applied for numerous types of misbehavior, such as disrespect and noncompliance. An *Effective Parent* uses time-out to assist a child in understanding the difference between acceptable and unacceptable behavior. ***Time-out*** provides an opportunity for a child to cease the disobedience while reflecting on his or her misbehavior for better decisions in the future.

A time-out assists your child in learning respect for your requests and rules, self-discipline, and good decision-making skills for obedient behavior. A time-out may also be used for a cool down period when a child is overwhelmed, distraught, and not able to gain control of his or her emotions. Most parents use the rule of thumb for time-outs as one minute for each year of age. Hence, a four-year old would go to time-out for four minutes.

Since the ultimate parenting goal is not control but to assist a child in growth toward obedience, I believe what teaches obedience best is to place the entire responsibility on the child. An alternative to the minute-per-age rule is to have your child say some form of the following phrases in order to leave time-out. First, the child must apologize, "I am sorry I did not listen. Will you please forgive me?" Second, "I am ready to obey and make better decisions."

Since apologizing and forgiving is absolutely essential for all relationships, the first statement and question accomplish that goal. You desire for your child to learn obedience and good decision-making skills, so the second part reinforces that tremendous objective. You decide what teaches obedience best for your child, the minute-per-age rule, the two phrases, or a combination of both.

The following guidelines can assist you in implementing time-out.

- ***Designate a location***. Select a location that isolates your child without any fun items such as a bathroom, hallway, corner of a room, or a laundry room. It is usually best to have your child sit during time-out.
- ***Request obedience***. Example, "*Will you please* be respectful?" Then, "*Either* be respectful *or* go to time-out, *you decide*."
- ***Be firm***. In a calm, firm manner send your child to time-out with "*You decided* to go to time-out *because* you continued to be disrespectful. You can *try again* after you *apologize* and are ready to make a better decision." Always tell your child what behavior was unacceptable.
- ***Don't give attention***. During time-out, your child should be alone, quiet, and not given any attention.
- ***Challenge continual misbehavior***. If your child is not calm and misbehaves during time-out, either remind the child of the apology and obedience statement or double the length of time based on the minute-per-age rule.
- ***Express love after time-out***. Do not lecture your child after time-out, but instead, verbally express your unconditional love for him or her as well as your faith in the child to be a great decision-maker.

Please note that children with sensory issues, autism, and Asperger's Syndrome may need something to self-soothe like a weighted blanket, favorite stuffed animal, or fiddle objects. Time-out is a wonderful method for teaching your child self-control and obedience. Certainly self-control, apologies, and excellent decision-making will enhance your child's future relationships along with successful societal functioning.

32. Spank

I like the word "spank" because it implies one swat on the bottom rather than "spanking" which infers numerous whacks on the bottom. A *spank* used appropriately and infrequently can be especially useful in reminding a child of a parent's leadership within the home, as well as securing obedience when a child displays exceedingly undesirable behavior. Please note that parents who frequently use ***spank*** as a first resort cause it to be less effective.

Some parents are hesitant to spank because they view a *spank* as violent discipline. Other individuals in society believe a *spank* is a form of abuse, but I disagree with both perspectives. Screaming with rage, hitting a child hard with an object, spanking a child numerous times, and a three-hour time-out for a five-year old, or any other form of extreme discipline is not only unhealthy but abuse. This kind of punitive discipline is emotionally painful and distorts a child's respect and love for his or her parent.

Knowing how and when to apply a successful ***spank*** can tremendously benefit a child in learning obedience. From eighteen months to two years, one gentle slap on the back of the hand is all that is needed to help a toddler better understand the word "No." For example, when a toddler touches the fireplace, an electrical outlet, or the oven, a parent needs to grab the child's immediate attention, letting the toddler know that such behavior is dangerous.

From two to eight years, an infrequent *spank* expresses a parent's disapproval of deliberate defiance or brazen disobedience.

Before the age of six, when a parent sensibly implements a spank, it will rarely be a discipline tool after six years of age.

After the age of eight, taking away a privilege or giving a logical consequence are the only forms of discipline, never a *spank*. A child receiving a *spank* after eight years of age often grows up with immense shame perhaps even feeling like a mistake or defect.

A *spank* is discipline that can be implemented for two reasons. First, *spank* when your child is determined to deliberately defy your parental guidance. Second, if possible bodily harm may occur for your child or another child, then *spank* him or her to teach responsible decision-making in harmful situations. The following guidelines can assist you in disciplining with a ***spank***.

- ***Spank as a last resort.*** Use *Will you please* and *Either/Or/You decide* before getting to the point of a spank. Only on rare occasions will a *spank* be the first discipline option.
- ***Absolutely never spank when you are upset or angry!*** Always be calm before giving a *spank* remembering your goal of obedience. Your child needs to feel he or she is receiving a *spank* because of your care and love.
- ***Only use your hand, never an object!*** Your goal is not to produce physical pain but only to secure your child's undivided attention over his or her flagrant misbehavior. You can also feel with your hand the impact of the *spank*.
- ***Deliver just one swat and only to the bottom.*** Never ever spank any other parts of the body. Furthermore, never cause significant physical pain with a *spank*.
- ***Before the spank, explain to your child the necessary reasons for your discipline.*** Be clear with your expectations for his or her future behavior.
- ***A spank should be administered in private, meaning, the bedroom or other room.*** A *spank* in front of others creates feelings of shame.

- ***After you spank, express your verbal and physical unconditional love for your child that you love him or her, no matter what.*** Your child must believe you only want what is best for his or her life.

Dispensed correctly, a ***spank*** is an immensely valuable tool for every parent to teach responsible behaviors. Closely follow the guidelines in this lesson to do it effectively and lovingly.

33. Never Say "I" and Avoid the Word "Punishment"

When the pronoun "*I*" is used by a parent a child usually feels the parent is controlling him or her. Whenever you share a consequence or take away privileges, never use the pronoun "I" because that infers you are in charge of your child's life, rather than your child making responsible decisions for his or her own life.

Per Lesson 29:

- Rather than saying, "*I am* sending you to time-out because you called your sibling a bad name," say instead, "***You decided*** to go to time-out ***because*** you called your sibling a bad name."
- Rather than saying, "*I am* taking away your cell phone because you have not cleaned your bedroom," say "***You decided*** to not have your cell phone ***because*** your bedroom is not yet clean."
- Rather than saying, "*I am* not letting you watch television because you did not finish your homework," say "***You decided*** to not watch television **because** of unfinished homework."

Many years ago, I counseled with a mom, a dad, and their thirteen-year-old son because of his severe behavior problems at home and school, poor academic performance, and extreme anger outbursts. I shared with both parents the importance of saying "***You decided***" when giving a consequence rather than "I." However, both parents seemed to enjoy controlling their son and continued beginning consequences with "I."

At a spring counseling session, the parents reported that *they were making* their son go to summer school because he failed his math class. Unfortunately, the parents told their son, "*We are making* you go to summer school to retake your math class." The thirteen-year old's anger was almost out of control over his parents stating, "*We are making* you . . ."

I met with the son in private and he continued raging over his parents' decision. In almost a whisper speaking low and slow I said, "Bob (not his real name), ***you decided*** to go to summer school." Intentionally, I did not give the reasons and use "***because***." Now he was also angry at me and told me it was his parents' fault. I made the same soft statement a second time, "Bob, ***you decided*** to go to summer school." He raised his upset voice and said, "Dr. Schroeder did you hear me, my parents are making me go to summer school."

I responded with that same statement almost thirty times in a low and slow voice. Finally, after about the thirtieth time of me saying, "Bob, ***you decided*** to go to summer school," Bob replied, "Dr. Schroeder you are right. *I decided* to go to summer school ***because*** I didn't do my homework and study for my tests." I wish I could write that his parents started using the *Effective Parenting* skills, but they did not. Sadly, the counseling ended, and their son eventually had serious problems with law enforcement.

Another critical tool is to ***never*** use the word "***punishment***." A person is punished to inflict hurt and pain in the hope of improvement. Criminals usually receive punishment for their crimes by going to prison. If a police officer gives you a ticket for speeding, his comment is not, "I am going to punish you by taking you to jail," but instead, "***You decided*** to receive a ticket ***because*** you were speeding." The police officer's goal is to help citizens obey the speed limit not to inflict pain.

Regrettably, many parents frequently use the word punishment and also begin with the pronoun "I" like, "I am going to punish you by . . ." At times, a parent who applies harsh, oppressive punishment is displacing personal anger onto his or her child.

Examples of harsh statements would be: "*I am punishing you* through time-out for calling your sibling a bad name," "*I am punishing you* by taking away your cell phone because you have not cleaned your bedroom," and "*I am punishing you* by not letting you watch television because you did not finish your homework." Do you understand how painful and unloving that would feel for a child?

Starting today, will you please *never* use the word "*punish*" or "*punishment*" because your child will probably interpret your statement as attempting to cause pain. No one likes to have torture inflicted upon him or her. If your child thinks that your goal is to cause agony, you will probably damage your parent-child relationship as well as produce an angry, rebellious child. Always use "***You decided . . . because***."

34. 3-Part Assertive Response

The *3-Part Assertive Response* is a tremendous tool for every *Effective Parent*. Flying off the handle by expressing excessive frustration erodes trust and damages leadership of your child. A major goal for every *Effective Parent* is to *pause, pause, pause* in order to not overreact. The *3-Part Assertive Response* will help you achieve that goal.

Every person wants to feel appreciated, valued, and special. Likewise, your child strongly desires to be cherished, respected, and treasured by you. One of the best ways to help your child feel important is with the ***3-Part Assertive Response***. If you are presently a parent, you probably have not played records. Records used to get "stuck" repeating the same thing over and over again. That originated the phrase "like a broken record." In a similar way, use the *3-Part Assertive Response* repeatedly especially when your child is upset. The three parts are:

1. ***Echo, Echo, Echo***: Reflect or repeat back to your child exactly each word he or she shares with you. Begin *echoing* back with the phrase "*I heard you say . . .*"
2. Use the word "***and,***" *never* "but". To keep your parent-child relationship whole, it is best to have run-on sentences by using the word "***and***." The word "but" is an eraser, a counter to what was said before the "but." No matter what follows the "but," a child will feel devalued and will not believe what his or her parent said before the "but."
3. Your ***response*** is what you think is *healthy* or in your child's *best interest*.

Here are two examples of the 3-Part Assertive Response:

Example 1

Child: "I want to watch television before doing my homework."

Parent: "***I heard you say*** you want to watch television before doing your homework ***and*** when your homework is finished then you may watch television" (healthy goal).

Example 2

Child: "I want to play video games for three hours on school nights."

Parent: "***I heard you say*** that you want to play video games for three hours on school nights ***and*** on school nights the guideline is a maximum of sixty minutes per night only after doing your homework" (healthy goal).

Years ago, my last counseling session on a Friday afternoon was with a single mom and her seventeen-year-old son who was often disrespectful as well as defiant. To say it nicely, his father was exceedingly unhealthy and did not set boundaries. I spent time individually with the mom and son. During my time with mom, I shared the *3-Part Assertive Response* and role played the response numerous times with her.

After the counseling session, I locked up the office and went toward my car. At the same time, I saw the seventeen-year-old burn rubber in the parking lot and speed away. Fortunately, the parking lot was fairly empty. The mom was standing by her car and began saying to me, "Thank you, thank you, thank you! My son asked to stay out till 3:00 a.m. with his friends and usually he wears me down and I eventually give in. I said to my son firmly yet kindly approximately ten times. '***I heard you say*** you want to stay out till 3:00 a.m. with your friends ***and*** your curfew is 12:30 a.m.' (best interest). After the tenth time, he knew I wasn't changing and frustrated he sped off." She began using the *3-Part Assertive Response* along with many other *Simple Habits* and that made an enormous difference in her son's respect and decision-making.

The ***3-Part Assertive Response*** is not a magical skill that produces a one hundred percent positive result every time. However, numerous *Effective Parents* have shared that this awesome *3-Part Assertive Response* has transformed their parenting approach in an encouraging direction.

35. Don't Reason and Don't Argue

In the history of the world, not one parent has ever won an argument with his or her child. Yet probably every parent in the world believes he or she can reason with his or her child and logically convince the child enough to win an argument. The Bible says, "When I was a child, I talked like a child, I thought like a child, I reasoned like a child" (1 Corinthians 13:11 NIV). God's Word is clearly telling parents, ***don't reason and don't argue***. You will not win!

When your child wants to argue, pull the plug out of the outlet so the "argument lamp light" does not go on. With the lamp plug out of the outlet, you could try to turn on the lamp until Jesus returns, but the "argument lamp light" is not going on. Children are unable to argue with their parents when parents simply refuse to argue with their children. To avoid devaluing your child along with escaping power struggles, memorize the following five phrases and speak them very softly and slowly:

1. I am sorry you feel that way.
2. I love you too much to argue with you.
3. I am sorry, if I were your age, I would probably have the same feeling about my parenting decision.
4. Will you please give us your reasons for thinking that is a good idea?
5. Will you please convince us why that is a healthy choice?

Through the age of ten, it is generally okay to give reasons for your decisions because younger children will accept the knowledge. For example, your child asks to have only chocolate cake for supper. You will probably respond, "***When you*** eat your chicken, fruits, and vegetables, ***then you*** may have a piece of cake but having only cake for supper is not healthy." Or your six-year-old child asks to play outside till 7:00 p.m. and then do homework. You will probably explain, "After dinner ***when you*** do your homework, ***then you*** may play outside, and your bedtime is 8:00 p.m."

However, after the age of ten, it is best not to reason with your child. For example, your sixteen-year-old asks to stay out until 3:00 a.m. You may have the wisdom of God with the finest reasons in the world for saying "no" like: "More people are drinking alcohol and driving after midnight and you might be hit by a drunk driver," or "After midnight, there are more predators who may bring you harm," or "The later you stay out after midnight, the more likely you will get into mischief." Your sixteen-year-old is not going to say, "Mom/dad those are wonderful reasons and I no longer want to stay out till 3:00 a.m." Such a response simply will never happen! Almost every sixteen-year-old would like to stay out until 3:00 a.m. if given the opportunity.

Instead, to help your sixteen-year-old feel valued, let your teen come up with the *reasons* why a 3:00 a.m. curfew is a good idea. Use questions like, "*Will you please* give us your ***reasons*** for thinking that a 3:00 a.m. curfew is a good idea?" Or "*Will you please* **convince us** why a 3:00 a.m. curfew is important?" If your teen responds, "The Youth Pastor and several parent chaperones are having a teen lock-in at church. The Youth Pastor plans to have a brief Bible study; order pizza for all the teens; play games in the gym followed by a movie; and finally, the Youth Pastor is taking all the teens home at 2:30 a.m. in the church bus." More than likely, you will now allow your teenager to have a 3:00 a.m. curfew because those are wonderful reasons. However, your teen came up with decent motives for a later curfew and there was no argument.

For the sake of your parent-child relationship and to ***avoid arguments***, implement regularly the five phrases you memorized.

36. Avoid Parent Deafness: Be Brief and Be Silent

Jesus at times made brief comments. When experiencing temptation, "Jesus answered him, 'It is also written: Do not put the Lord your God to the test'" (Matthew 4:7 NIV). Before calming the storm, "He (Jesus) replied, 'You of little faith, why are you so afraid'" (Matthew 8:26 NIV)?

Parents would do well to follow Jesus' example by being *brief*. Many parents have the misconception that lectures will tremendously benefit their child in learning obedience. Please understand you may give the best lecture in the world but, after five seconds, your child has completely turned off the volume and hears nothing. Talking too much or discussing a situation forever leads a child to practice ***parent deafness***.

I once knew an attorney who was extremely successful in negotiating contracts for a major corporation. Although this attorney was a petite woman, she capably stood toe-to-toe with two or three opposing lawyers during negotiations and was almost always successful in achieving the best deal for her corporation.

One day, I asked the attorney her secret, she simply replied in one word, "Silence." When asked for an explanation, the attorney responded, "I briefly state my requirements and then remain silent while the other attorneys argue back and forth and try to change my mind. In the end, my silence exhausts them and they give in to my demands. My philosophy is, the lawyer who is the briefest, and more importantly most silent, is the attorney who wins the negotiation."

Likewise, as a parent, keep your words to a minimum by being ***brief*** and ***silent***. How do you discipline with a few words? Use the tools *Either/Or/You decide* and *When you/Then you* along with other parenting tools found in this chapter. Those excellent verbal judo skills will provide you with the ability to overcome ***parent deafness***.

Another fantastic *brief* strategy is the *one-word* skill that follows a *will you please* after a lack of obedience. Some examples of what you might say to your child are:

"*Will you please* be respectful?" But when it does not happen, say kindly "respect," meaning be respectful.

"*Will you please* place your dishes in the sink?" But when it does not happen, firmly say "dishes," insinuating to remove the dishes from the table.

"*Will you please* place your shoes in the closet?" But when it does not happen, decisively say "shoes," implying put your shoes in the closet.

Always remember to praise your child for his or her good decision, as well as accomplishing a responsibility with an "I appreciate . . ." The *one-word* tool will also allow you to evaluate how well you are leading your child toward obedient choices. When your child makes a good decision with only a *one-word* correction following a *will you please*, feel good about your parenting and your child's obedient decision-making.

Few words, not many, will assist you in avoiding *parent deafness* so you can lead your child to become a responsible decision-maker. An *Effective Parent* strives for obedience with ***briefness***, ***silence***, and the ***one-word skill***.

37. Save Your "NOs" for What Matters

Please understand that a healthy balance must be maintained between your "Yes" and "No" parenting decisions. Most desires by your child are not life or death. Many parenting decisions will also not have a significant impact on the outcome of your child's life. Hence, it is important to differentiate your child's minor requests from major ones.

When a child makes a request, some parents say "No" too quickly without considering if the request is simply insignificant or important. A controlling or overprotective parent has great difficulty in loosening the reins on the child and, sadly, "No" usually predominates the parent's guidance. A parent who controls with an abundance of "NOs" causes his or her child to feel trapped with freedom as a distant reality.

At times, for your benefit and the sake of your child, say "Yes." Per Chapter One, rules and routines are healthy for a child; however, rigid rules and inflexibility will harm a parent-child relationship. For example, your child asks for an extra 30 to 45 minutes to play a video game. Say "Yes" every so often. Or your child wants to play an extra thirty minutes before starting homework, say "Yes" sometimes. Or after playing outside for a couple of hours, your child asks for an extra dessert in the afternoon, giving another "Yes" should be fine. All these examples are inconsequential in terms of impacting your child's adult life.

On the other hand, if a fifteen-year-old requests a curfew of 2:00 a.m., a "Yes" could lead to significant problems if there isn't a plan like a two-hour bus ride from a sports activity. Or if a four-year-old asks to ride his or her big wheels in the street, a "Yes" has the potential for serious physical harm. Or a ten-year-old wants to ride a bike to a shopping mall five miles away, a "Yes" has potential negative consequences.

As a parent, you promote goodwill when you can say "Yes" to simple requests allowing for exceptions to the rule. Every child wants the freedom to be in charge of his or her own life. Freedom comes with limits but expand those boundaries by granting wishes whenever possible so your child can one day function independently as an adult.

Whenever you must say "No" to your child's requests, remember the importance of your facial expression and tone of voice. Definitely, your child needs to know you don't take pleasure in having to say "No." An *Effective Parent* communicates empathy and sensitivity that saying "No" is hard, but you simply are concerned for the child's well-being. State your firm and friendly "No" in such a way your child understands that answer is in his or her best interests because you love him or her.

Always remember that it is okay to say "No," but don't do it too quickly, and say "Yes" when the circumstances are appropriate. A good rule of thumb is to reserve your ***"No" for those times that really matter,*** and say "Yes" with minor requests to demonstrate love and care for your child.

38. Is This an Emergency?

Lower your expectations and understand your child will make mistakes just like you commit life missteps. Most situations are also not life and death. Yet, the human tendency is to reply immediately with even minor troubling situations. The adage is so true, "Bite your tongue." Hence, never overreact when your child makes a mistake. Act wisely, do not react poorly!

Since every word you speak can "make or break" your child's spirit, don't make rushed comments that you might regret because you lost self-control. Responding in anger will only hurt your goal of guiding and teaching your child. Don't handle your child's troubles when you are emotional. Even something as serious as being late for curfew can be handled best the next day.

Always think PAUSE, PAUSE, and PAUSE! Then ask, "***Is this situation an emergency?***" Ninety-nine percent of the time the answer is "No." Numerous parents have told me that asking themselves, "*Is this an emergency?*" has helped them remain composed and respectful. By waiting fifteen minutes, thirty minutes or maybe even a day, it will be so much easier to speak calmly and logically in a ***low and slow*** voice.

When your child has a major request, asking yourself, "*Is this an emergency?*" can be valuable. Besides thinking of that question to provide an unrushed answer, another way to take your time and not respond immediately is to say, "*Please let me think about your request.*"

I counseled with a dad who struggled with anger and had a disrespectful teenage son. The dad's emotional outbursts toward his son only damaged their relationship and reinforced the son's problem behavior. I will never forget the dad telling me: "Using '*Is this an emergency?*' was an enormous factor in handling my anger, being a better parent, and helping my son make better decisions. I almost always wait till the next day to address a major issue." What happened? The dad's relationship with his son immensely improved.

Your ultimate goal is to instruct and guide your child to be a better decision-maker so he or she will be a responsible adult one day. So next time your child commits a major misbehavior, ask yourself, "***Is this an emergency*** that must be handled right now?" or "Can I wait until I have more self-control?"

39. Don't Get Defensive with "I Don't Like You" or "This Is Not Fair"

The prodigal son basically told his father something like, "I don't like you or this home environment. I can enjoy life a lot more on my own." (Luke 15:11-32). Although the son was rebellious, the father of the prodigal son was wonderful, gave unconditional love, and did not take his son's selfishness and greed personally.

Likewise, avoid getting defensive and having your feelings hurt when your child pushes your buttons with "I don't like you" or the major button "I hate you." At some point, those comments or similar remarks are made by almost every child, so expect that to happen. For a child under ten, that feeling may last one or two hours and for a teenager that emotion may last a day.

Do not overreact to those phrases or anything that your child says to you by getting defensive and flying off the handle. An aggressive response is detrimental and will only increase the frequency of disrespectful comments. Instead, remain calm and remember, "I am leading my child to become a responsible decision-maker. My child made a mistake, and this is a learning opportunity."

View these upsetting comments as teaching moments to support your child in learning respect for you and others even when they are hurtful. Make statements or ask questions like, "We love each other. How would you feel if I spoke to you that way?" And, "Please tell me in a respectful way what I specifically said or did that bothers you." And eventually, "Will you please apologize for what you said?" When your child is unhappy with you, have a goal to assist your child with acquiring self-control. As an adult, your child will need to demonstrate restraint with others, his or her spouse, and perhaps with his or her own children.

Finally, your child will frequently say, "This is not fair," regarding situations both inside and outside your home. That comment will be made hundreds of times before your child finishes high school, and how often do we, as adults, have that thought.

Perhaps one of the very first foundational principles your child needs to learn is that "Life is not fair and something unfair will happen almost every day."

When your child says "This is not fair," about a parenting decision, relax, smile on the inside, and say to yourself, "I probably made the correct decision because my child just said, 'This is not fair.'" And as a parent, you probably should keep doing what you said or did.

Parental preparation for possible challenges is extremely important. As an *Effective Parent*, plan for how you will handle those two phrases, "I don't like you" and "This is not fair."

40. Five Fantastic Guidelines for Important Talks

Whenever you have an important topic or problem to discuss with your child you want to absolutely have predetermined discussion guidelines. Perhaps, begin each important talk by praying with your child for a respectful discussion while searching for answers. Five fantastic guidelines that also make a dramatic positive difference in your important talks are:

1. After 9:00 a.m. and before 7:00 p.m.
2. Always sit
3. Avoid "why"
4. Speak low and slow
5. Speak the truth in love

After 9:00 a.m. and before 7:00 p.m. Ecclesiastes 3:1 encourages, "There is a time for everything" (NIV), including never having an important talk before 9:00 a.m. and after 7:00 p.m. Feelings are delicate early in the morning and late at night, when discussions can quickly escalate into arguments. Fatigue creates little tolerance for frustration. Rarely, if ever, will a parent have a respectful, productive talk with the child before 9:00 a.m. and after 7:00 p.m. Be flexible with this guideline. Some parents wait to have a discussion with their child until after 10:00 a.m. or even 11:00 a.m. Other parents do not have a serious talk with their child after 6:00 p.m. Come up with times that work best for your family.

Always sit. When a person stands, it is difficult for him or her to listen well. In addition, there is a greater likelihood that the conversation will rapidly become a shouting match. Standing is an intimidating posture especially for a child. Being seated also allows you to be at eye level with your child.

With every important "talk," always sit down with your child. Perhaps, the best place to sit is the kitchen table, similar to the business model of sitting at a conference table. The goal of looking for solutions to the problem seems to happen best when a parent and child sit at the kitchen table. If the kitchen table does not work, find another location, but always be seated.

Avoid "why." Whenever the word "why" is used, that automatically feels like an attack and implies that the motives of the other person were wrong. Instead of asking your child "why" use the question, "What are (were) your reasons?"

Speak low and slow. Begin your important talk with a volume that is just above a whisper. It is always easy to increase your volume, but whenever a parent starts loud, it is almost impossible to decrease volume. Remember what the Bible says, "A ***soft*** and gentle and thoughtful answer turns away wrath" (Proverbs 15:1 AMP). And, "Let everyone be quick to hear [be a careful, thoughtful listener], ***slow*** to speak [a speaker of carefully chosen words]" (James 1:19 AMP).

Begin with Speak the truth in love. *Speak the truth in love* is a direct quote found in Ephesians 4:15 and is simply an expansion of the "I" message, a respectful way to express your expectations or concerns to your child. The goal is to avoid beginning a sentence with the pronoun "you," which is attacking and blaming. The *Speak the truth in love* assertion has the following four parts:

1. "***When I heard***" (involving what was said) or "***When I saw***" (involving actions).
2. "***I felt hurt***" or "***I felt disappointed***" or if it was deeply troubling, "***I felt hurt and disappointed.***" NEVER use the barrier words angry, frustrated, mad, upset, infuriated, livid, etc. Those barrier words will place an emotional wall between you and your child.
3. "***Because,***" provide ***reasons*** for your hurt and disappointment.
4. "***Will you please,***" offer a ***solution(s)*** to your hurt and disappointment.

On a school day around 3:30 pm, I was counseling a mom to help her positively influence her struggling ten-year old son. She received a call on her cell phone and immediately recognized it was a school number. The principal was calling to inform this mom her son had just gotten in trouble on the school bus ride home.

She was angry, ready to go home, and lecture her son about his misbehavior. I calmed her down and suggested a different approach. I advised, "After your son arrives home around 4:15 p.m., ask, "***Will you please*** sit at the kitchen table and have some cookies and milk?" After he finishes his cookies and milk say to him, "***When I heard*** the principal tell me that you got in trouble on the school bus, ***I felt hurt and disappointed because*** that is not like you, you are better than that. ***Will you please*** respect the bus driver and behave on the bus?" In my office, she practiced saying that exact *Speak the truth in love* statement several times.

At the next counseling session, she smiled and reported an incredibly positive discussion with her son. I continued to counsel with this mom for the remainder of the school year. I am very happy to write that her son never got in trouble on the bus again and his classroom behavior was also commendable. I genuinely believe that, had this mom given a yelling lecture, the outcome for her son's school year would have been more negative.

Another example was a seventeen-year-old who tried snorting cocaine with his friends. This young man's parents found out from other parents and immediately came to me for counseling. I suggested they use the *Speak the truth in love* assertive response. I recommended they say, "***When we heard*** that you tried cocaine, ***we felt really hurt and disappointed because*** that is not like you, you are better than that and cocaine is extremely harmful and can damage your entire life. ***Will you please*** never use cocaine again?"

The next day, I met with the son. When I asked him, "Will you ever try cocaine again?" He instantly said, "Never." I asked, "What are your reasons?" (not "Why?") He immediately replied, "My mom and dad told me they were ***really hurt and disappointed.*** I never want to hurt and disappoint my parents like that again." Please note that responses like this teenager's comment are built on a foundation of love and trust that started when he was much younger. Of course, I did not share I had provided his parents with the assertive *Speak the truth in love* response. I honestly believe if these parents had a shouting lecture with their son, while at the same time using the *barrier words*, there would have been a negative outcome with more drug use.

Every Friday night, there are numerous teenagers late for curfew, and of course, it will be after 7:00 p.m. *Effective Parents* will meet their teenager at the door disappointed and hurt at their teen's poor decision to not be home on time.

Unfortunately, many parents will confront their teen after the 7:00 p.m. guideline with, "*Why* were you late?" In addition, the parents and their teenager are standing, not sitting. If the lateness was addressed at that very moment, almost always the parents and their teenager will escalate the discussion into a huge, ugly argument with fast speech and loud voices. Then, both teenager and parents will probably go to bed mad and frustrated with one another. And the angry teenager may make it a goal to either not get caught next time or be even more rebellious in the future.

What is the healthier way to handle that "missing curfew" situation? Based upon the ***Five Fantastic Guidelines***, an *Effective Parent* will meet the teenager at the door and, in front of the teenager, look at their watch without saying one word just to confirm the teen was late for curfew. Then, an *Effective Parent* will tell the teen to have a good night's sleep and go to bed. As a parental leader in the home, the parent(s) will sleep very well. However, the teen will probably squirm all night, not sleep at all, and obsessively wonder what is going to happen the next morning.

On Saturday morning, parents can easily prepare their response as they focus on goals for dealing with this situation. After 9:00 a.m. the next morning, an *Effective Parent* will ask his or her teenager, "*Will you please* sit at the kitchen table with me (us)?" After the parents and their teenager are sitting at the kitchen table, *Effective Parents* will say in a low and slow voice the *Speak the truth in love words:* "***When we saw*** that you were late for curfew last night, ***we felt*** very hurt and disappointed ***because*** we were very worried about you and you could have easily called us (me) on your cell phone. ***Will you please*** help us understand your reasons for being late for curfew last night?" With high probability, this important discussion at the kitchen table will be significantly better than if the parents had engaged the teenager with everyone standing very late at night.

Another example of the importance of the ***Five Fantastic Guidelines*** is a fourteen-year-old and his parents who I counseled. One school day around 7:45 a.m., the mom, frantic and crying hysterically, called because her fourteen-year-old son had just shoved her and screamed at her. I calmly asked the mom two rhetorical questions, "What time is it? Did you bring up a sensitive, serious topic?"

Immediately after my two questions, she recognized her poor decision which included breaking the guideline *after 9:00 a.m.*

and before 7:00 p.m. with important topics or problems. I suggested she drop the discussion, take her son to school, and tell him "I love you so much and hope you have a very nice day!" I then suggested, "After you pick your son up from school, be encouraging and say nothing in the car about the morning conflict. Once you arrive home ask, "***Will you please*** sit at the kitchen table?" and give him milk and a snack. After he finishes his snack, use the *Speak the truth in love* formula to address your concern.

Next day at her counseling session, the mom happily reported that she followed my suggestions, and their discussion went extremely well. This mom also shared that her son had two tests that day and a short speech to present. It was no wonder that he was impatient and had such a short fuse. Please realize that I am not excusing the son's disrespectful actions. This mom found it easier to forgive her son when he described his day, and most importantly, she recognized that the argument was really due to her not following the *Five Fantastic Guidelines*. I genuinely believe she rarely broke the guidelines again.

Always know that the very best time to have any type of important talk is when you and your child are both relaxed and not emotional. Furthermore, the best way to solve problems happens when you, as a parent, listen well with your ears and eyes. Through implementation of the ***Five Fantastic Guidelines***, you can have wonderful discussions with your child, while being a patient, compassionate listener.

41. Listen Effectively: Ask Open-Ended "How" and "What" Questions

Jesus asked 307 questions because that was a central aspect of his teaching. Socrates also used "**How**" and "**What**" questions to impart knowledge with others. Experienced educators use the Socratic method to instruct their students because that is much more beneficial than boring lectures.

As a parent, you could present the very best lecture in the world and, after five seconds, your child has tuned you out. *Effective Parents* are much further ahead by asking questions that begin with "How" and "What," when they are instructing their child, especially on serious topics. Again, remember not to ask "Why" questions because that builds a barrier between you and your child.

An example of utilizing "How" and "What" questions would be speaking with your teenager regarding sexuality and the importance of respecting future marriage. Some valuable questions might be:

- ***What*** are the benefits of waiting for marriage?
- ***How*** are you respecting your future spouse by not having sexual intercourse now?
- ***What*** diseases are possible through sexual activity?
- ***How*** special will your honeymoon and marriage be when you do not have intercourse before your wedding day?
- ***What*** happens to your self-worth when you avoid sexual intercourse before marriage?

Like Jesus and Socrates, probably the best way to guide and instruct your child is through "How" and "What" questions. You enter your child's world through loving questions and great listening. When you ***ask questions*** and ***listen well,*** you discover the deepest thoughts of your child's heart that lead to a wonderful parent-child relationship.

42. Gradually Allow Your Child to Make Decisions

While under a parent's supervision, a child needs to take responsibility for his or her choices at home because that will prepare him or her for choices in society. From an early age, teach your child that quality of life is dependent on decision-making and making the right choices. As an adult, some major life decisions your child may face are:

- Career
- College
- Spouse
- Where to live
- Type of home
- Seeking a new job
- Choosing Christian friends
- Financial budgeting

A significant *Effective Parenting* goal is to assist your child in becoming a great decision-maker. Always have faith in your child's maturing wisdom and regularly express a belief in his or her abilities to make good choices. As your child grows and demonstrates positive decision-making, increase his or her privileges and the amount of his or her choices.

A word of caution is necessary with decision-making opportunities for your child. In life, extremes are generally not healthy, and moderation or balance is the goal. An extreme parent who allows the child too many choices at an early age encourages a child to be too independent. This type of parenting can develop a strong-willed child who may refuse to listen to his or her parents.

I have counseled many parents who understood the importance of decision-making opportunities but went overboard by having their child make decisions about nearly everything. Too many choices created struggles for their child starting as young as three. Offering too many decisions produced a defiant child who thought he or she was in total charge of his or her life. Parents taking it to the extreme with too many choices have reported that their child doesn't listen well, wants to make all the decisions and wishes the parents would simply back off.

There is nothing wrong with asking a young child, "Would you rather wear blue socks or black socks?" "Would you rather have toast or a bagel?" "Would you rather have milk or orange juice?" However, giving your child choices with almost every aspect of his or her life will only lead to a strong-minded child through the teen years.

There is no objective measure for a correct number of choices. Based upon your child's age and abilities, provide decision-making opportunities with aspects of his or her life. As your child grows older, gradually increase decision-making opportunities rather than curtail choices. Just make sure that your child understands you are the leader, and you will make final decisions not your child. ***Gradually allow your child to make choices*** so he or she will successfully generate responsible decisions as an adult one day.

43. Three "I" Words: Immoral, Illegal, or Irreversible

Some parents set boundaries on a child's decisions that really do not impact his or her adult life. Frequently, a parent will ask me in counseling, "Should I let my child do this or do that?" I almost always recommend the ***three "I" words***. To guide a parent's thought process, I recommend a parent ask, "Is my child's choice ***immoral, illegal, or irreversible***?" If the answer is "No," then as a parent you might let your child make that choice.

For example, when I was younger, I wore my hair over my ears. My parents were not happy with my choice. However, "Was it *immoral or illegal* for me to wear my hair longer?" Of course, the answer is no. Today, I am balding, so my decision was definitely not *irreversible* either.

Today, many adults have tattoos, so I am not writing negatively against tattoos, only using that as an example. If a thirteen-year-old child asks a parent to get a tattoo, the question would be, "Is it *immoral, illegal, or irreversible* to get a tattoo at thirteen?" Certainly, it is not immoral, but as I am writing this book, it is

illegal for a person to receive a tattoo in most states unless he or she is sixteen years old. In addition, a tattoo is somewhat ***irreversible*** because it is difficult to remove. If a thirteen-year-old asks, "May I have a tattoo?" A parent can easily say no because tattoos for a thirteen-year-old are ***illegal*** and ***irreversible***.

Please understand that the *three "I" words* may not apply to every major decision. However, the ***three "I" words: immoral, illegal, or irreversible***, can definitely be of assistance as you evaluate the pros and cons of your child's requests. The *three "I" words* also allow you to focus on important aspects of your child's life that more greatly impact his or her adulthood.

CHAPTER 4

HABITS THAT ESTABLISH AN ENCOURAGING ATMOSPHERE

Our world today is dramatically different than it was even one generation ago. Due to technology, adults and children face so many more temptations than in previous generations. Sadly, there also seems to be fewer positive, Biblically-principled role models that can be inspiring for your child.

One of the purposes of this chapter is to help you understand the importance of providing an encouraging atmosphere for your child. Whatever the family atmosphere, like a sponge, your child will absorb both positive qualities and negative aspects. Hence, the "family air" will play a major role in shaping your child's character and future adult life. These ideas will equip you to be more encouraging than discouraging, as well as be proactive not reactive with your interactions.

44. An Attitude of Gratitude

One of the greatest skills you can learn to master is the skill of gratitude. The Bible encourages, "Give thanks in all circumstances" (1 Thessalonians 5:18 NIV). Teaching your child to live every day gratefully begins with your ***attitude of gratitude***.

"I am entitled" has become the mantra for a large segment of society today. Sadly, the adage, "There is no such thing as a free lunch," has now also become a false belief. Being around a person who feels entitled is a miserable experience because he or she is so ungrateful. Likewise, a child with feelings of entitlement is often envious, lazy, and ungrateful. Sadly, for an entitled child enough is simply never enough and he or she is continually unhappy.

Life satisfaction comes from achievements that require self-sacrifice and hard work. Part of the accomplishment process is experiencing frustration mixed with gratification. The practice of living gratefully often flows out of adversity and disappointment. Think of the apostle Paul with all his struggles, "beaten with rods, stoned, shipwrecked three times" (2 Corinthians 11:25). Nonetheless, the apostle Paul had an attitude of gratitude and began his letters to fellow believers in Christ with praise and thanksgiving.

Frustration and delayed gratification will strengthen your child's character traits. Teach your child how to live gratefully by possessing a thankful heart for even the little things in life. Raise your child to understand the significance of being grateful for what you have. Having regular responsibilities helps your child become grateful for opportunities to support the family home.

What is one major way to motivate your child? Have an attitude of gratitude yourself! Rarely use the "Cs," criticism, complaints, and condemnation, around your child, which sap the life out of gratitude. Gratitude is something you cannot show too much and often enough. On a regular basis, express gratitude to others in front of your child.

The two words "terrible" and "terrific" are opposite in their meaning and yet the only difference in those words are the last three letters. Please tell your child regularly he or she has a *terrific* attitude and watch his or her grateful spirit also improve.

You can also model an *attitude of gratitude* by frequently telling your child, "Thank you." Encourage your child to appreciate life by saying "Thank you" often and expressing gratitude for the little things in life.

Let your *attitude of gratitude* build your child up in every aspect of life. A leadership parent is intentional in living life with a thankful heart and I believe you will be terrific at that goal!

45. Smiles, Laughter, And Humor

Never taking life or yourself too seriously is an important goal both personally and for your family. Cheerfulness, smiles, humor, and laughter are excellent stress-busters for every family. The Bible affirms, "A happy heart is good medicine and a joyful mind causes healing, But a broken spirit dries up the bones" (Proverbs 17:22 AMP). Proverbs 15:15 declares, "For the happy heart, life is a continual feast" (NLT).

This world can be negative and even somewhat grim at times. One of the best coping mechanisms is a sense of humor. What improves physical health and stimulates the mind is a joyful, cheerful spirit coupled with laughter. Strive to lighten up and let your child observe you joking around, having fun, and expressing humorous interaction.

A smile is one of the most important skills a parent can utilize. Almost nothing will warm your child's heart as when you smile at him or her. A smile inspires confidence, understanding, and care for your child. A smiling, encouraging parent positively influences, compared with a gloom-and-doom parent. How often do you smile at your child? Start smiling and smile a lot!

Laughing together with your child is also greatly beneficial. Key question: How often do you laugh in your home? Regularly laugh and laugh a lot! However, when your child has a setback or embarrassing moment, never laugh at your child because that significantly devalues his or her self-worth.

Think of ways to add fun and cheerfulness to your family atmosphere. ***Smiles, laughter, and humor*** are wonderful assets for your family. Laughing and enjoying life together is essential for all family members, particularly your child.

46. Lovingly Speak with Your Pet

Your body language and tone of voice are extremely powerful influencers upon your child's emotional well-being. You demonstrate the most respect through your facial expression and sound of your voice. Studies have found that your words are only about ten percent of your message, while tone and body language are approximately ninety percent.

Speak to your child with a warm, caring tone of voice. A young child is much like a puppy in that he or she hears tone of voice and sees body language without recognizing all the words. A dog never understands your words, only your *body language and tone of voice*. For example, if you said very softly and lovingly, "You are a vicious, brutal, and extremely mean beast." The dog would wag its tail with delight. On the other hand, if you moved your hand in an up and down motion and brashly or forcefully said, "You are a kind and caring pet." The dog would cower down for fear of being hit or yelled at. Thus, the dog never heard your words, only your ***tone of voice*** and ***body language***.

Likewise, speak to your child in the same gentle way you would speak to a pet. Definitely, your *tone and body language* speak volumes about your ongoing attitude toward your child. A soft, loving voice combined with a caring facial expression will create within your child the belief that you respect him or her and purposefully are parenting in every way for his or her benefit. On the other hand, if your volume is loud coupled with a disturbed demeanor, you will be devaluing to your child.

There is nothing wrong with being forceful with your tone when needed, but do not have an angry facial expression. On the other hand, when you are loud with an unkind expression, you come across as disrespectful and almost uncaring, leading your child to avoid listening to your guidance. Whenever you speak with your child, slow down, exhibit self-control, and remember your words are the least important part of your message.

Please note the one time your words are ninety percent of the message is when you say something about your child to another person. Your child seems to believe that almost one hundred percent of whatever you say about them to someone else is your genuine perspective of him or her. Negative examples would be telling another person in the child's presence that he or she is disorganized or shy or anxious or a poor student. Those labels are devastating for your child personally, plus you significantly weaken your relationship with your child. At all times speak positively about your child to others because that validates how proud you are of him or her.

Always remember, your ***body language and tone of voice*** make a world of difference in your child's trust and respect for you. In addition, a positive facial expression coupled with a caring tone will enhance your child's self-worth along with the belief that you have his or her best interests at heart.

47. Compliment More Than You Correct

Many loving parents believe that what leads to a child becoming a responsible decision-making adult is determined by how often a parent uses the "Cs": correction and criticism of wrongful behavior. A parent constantly following the "Cs" approach is unintentionally breaking a child's spirit, which produces discouragement, low self-worth, and a lack of self-confidence. And often, a child who frequently experiences the "Cs" wonders, "Do my parents believe in me?" or "Do my parents even think I am capable in life?" Many adults have shared in counseling a statement like, "My parents were so critical of me that I had a very difficult time believing my parents were sincere when they gave me a compliment."

There is also a misunderstanding that one unhelpful correction or criticism can be countered by just one compliment. Unfortunately, it is not a simple one-to-one ratio that will bring the emotional love bank account back to a breakeven. Studies have found that for every negative "C" given a child, a parent needs to deliver somewhere between five to nine compliments in order to balance that correction or criticism.

The apostle Paul frequently thanked and praised fellow believers throughout his thirteen books of the New Testament. Your child also needs support and encouragement, which comes more through compliments. Properly raising a child involves giving more compliments than corrections. Jesus taught and encouraged more than he corrected, causing his disciples to follow Him. Focus more on *catching your child doing things right* and praising those behaviors or words, because that makes a significant difference in his or her self-worth and future decision-making.

An example of too much correction and criticism is a twenty-year old young man I counseled for low self-esteem and poor decision-making skills. This twenty-year old said that his dad "always criticized almost everything he did" and rarely complimented or praised him. In fact, I asked if his dad ever said he was proud of him and the young man immediately replied, "Never." This twenty-year-old said when he was twelve, he pitched an entire Little League baseball game. He struck out 15 of 18 batters and went four-for-four as a hitter. After playing an unbelievable baseball game, he said his dad criticized him for not striking out all 18 batters and said absolutely nothing about his tremendous hitting performance. No wonder this young man struggled in so many ways including a lack of self-confidence and low self-worth.

On the positive side, I counseled a dad whose son played on a state high school championship football team. The dad reported that his son had a fantastic experience because the new coach of the team stressed the importance of *compliments more than corrections*.

In one game, this state championship team was down at half-time by two touchdowns and not playing well. The son was surprised the head coach did not address the team at halftime but spoke to all the assistant coaches. The head coach in essence told the assistant coaches, "When our players are coming off the field, all of you are just correcting and complaining about how our players are performing. Knock it off!!! In the second half, all I want to hear is compliments and praise for the tremendous effort our players are giving."

What happened? The assistant coaches started giving the players compliments and praise for what they were doing right in the game. This championship football team won the game by three touchdowns. What made the difference, *compliments and praise*! Like the coach, the dad began taking an approach of focusing even more on compliments than corrections.

Compliments and praise are one of the most important aspects of parenting. ***Praise and compliments*** are powerful and create energy within your child to make even more responsible decisions. Daily, an essential goal is to search for ways to compliment your child!

48. Praise Publicly, Correct Privately

Certainly, the cliche "praise publicly, correct privately" has been around forever and is used both in the business world as well as in family relationships. No one wants to be corrected in public! The Bible encourages, "Let no corrupting talk come out of your mouths, but only such as is good for building up, as fits the occasion, that it may give grace to those who hear" (Ephesians 4:29 ESV).

Every person is sinfully flawed and that makes it so amazingly easy to be a faultfinder rather than a good finder. Finding fault with a child in public is certainly not a blessing. Although a challenge, praising is always the number one goal before correcting. Praise in both private and public but *only correct in private*!

Sadly, in public settings, I have witnessed parents joke about weaknesses by making fun of how their child pronounces words, laughs, runs, struggles in school, acts clumsy, etc.

Doubly devastating is making cruel corrections or discouraging comments to a child in front of others. A parent publicly making fun of or correcting a child absolutely demoralizes that child and destroys his or her emotional well-being. Parents who condemn or correct publicly are probably more viciously critical at home, producing within a child anxiety, depression, lack of confidence, and incredibly low self-esteem.

In today's world, another big danger for correcting publicly is social media. NEVER shame or humiliate your child through a public social media forum.

In my counseling practice, I have seen a lot of heartache when a parent, grandparent, family member, or friend embarrasses a child on social media, whether intentionally or unintentionally. This is not just correcting publicly in front of a few people, but humiliating a child in various ways before countless people. In some cases, such emotional damage may last a lifetime. Definitely, be cautious with bragging through social media, BUT never share any negative information about your child.

In a public setting with others, do not correct table manners, poor grammar, behavioral flaws, etc. Wait until there is either an opportunity at home or take your child to a somewhat private area to make the correction. When you need to correct your child, ALWAYS do it in private!

Proverbs 3:27 provides great wisdom, "Do not hold back anything good from those who are entitled to it when you have the power to do so" (GW). That means complimenting and praising your child publicly! It means proudly introducing your child to others in public with a loving tone of voice that says my child is special, wonderful, and valued. ***Praising publicly*** and ***correcting privately*** will build a strong parent-child relationship, enhance your child's self-worth, and communicate to your child that you are so incredibly grateful to be his or her parent.

49. Never Be Sarcastic

Tied closely to *praise publicly and correct privately* is the importance of avoiding every form of sarcasm. In the Greek language, the word for sarcasm means "tearing of flesh." When a child has his or her emotional flesh torn, that is painful, especially by a parent. Every parent wants to be encouraging; however, sarcasm has the opposite effect and is extremely discouraging.

Often unknowingly, a parent will be sarcastic, tease, lightheartedly ridicule, all in the name of having fun with his or her child. ***Body language sarcasm*** such as rolling the eyes, a contemptuous smile, etc. can be equally as harmful as ***verbal sarcasm***. Any sarcasm is an emotional slap to a child.

Colossians 3:21 reminds parents, "Fathers (mothers), do not embitter your children, or they will become discouraged" (NIV). Frequently, a child with low self-worth usually has one or both parents make regular sarcastic comments to him or her.

Sarcasm is like giving your child ice cream and then pouring on vinegar as a topping. No matter how good the ice cream, the vinegar will make the ice cream taste horrible. Likewise, with sarcasm, it hurts when your child is the butt of the joke. No matter how good the humor, your child will feel horrible on the inside.

Proverbs 12:18 encourages, "There is one whose rash words are like sword thrusts, but the tongue of the wise brings healing" (ESV). A parent's words need to "bring healing" with toppings of words that are like chocolate syrup and whipped cream, not vinegar comments.

Sarcasm and ***cynicism*** lower self-esteem in a heartbeat!

Sarcasm not only stifles communication, but it is also destructive to relationships, including a parent-child connection. Parental sarcasm is an emotional bee sting that inflicts pain on a child. The consequence is, a child feels stupid or senseless.

When a parent uses any form of sarcasm, that almost automatically diminishes respect and trust for a child with his or her parent. The toxic weapon of sarcasm weakens, not strengthens, a parent-child bond. That often leads to discouragement creating reluctance for a child to reach out to his or her parent in the future.

A child is usually hesitant to share hurts and disappointments with a parent when he or she thinks the response will be sarcastic. Belittling a child often creates a deep fear in the child to disclose any feelings and thoughts with the parent, not only about small worries, but sadly, important life concerns as well.

Whenever a parent brings the child to counseling for anxiety, depression, low self-worth, poor effort, etc., one of the first questions I ask is, "How often does either parent use sarcasm, subtle put-downs, or ridicule?" Hundreds of times I have heard a parent sadly reply, "Frequently."

I kindly, gently explain how devastating sarcasm is for the child. Then, I ask that the parent *never* use any form of sarcasm ever again. I am amazed how quickly a child's self-esteem can be improved when parents cease using ***sarcasm, whether verbal or body language,*** with their child.

Avoiding sarcasm is critical for a child's emotional well-being and relational connection with the parent. Every person needs to use encouraging speech, as Ephesians 4:29 suggests, "Don't say anything that would hurt another person. Instead, speak only what is good so that you can give help wherever it is needed. That way, what you say will help those who hear you" (GW).

Words can build up but words can also tear down! Every comment a parent makes to a child is either valuing or devaluing! Words can make a child emotionally ill, just as words can make a child feel confident, optimistic, and safe under the parents' care. An *Effective Parent absolutely avoids every form of sarcasm!*

50. Your Expectations Impact Your Child

What you ***expect*** of your child functions as a self-fulfilling prophecy. When you have high expectations for your child, your child will have high expectations for himself or herself, as well. Expect your child to be respectful, expect your child to do chores, expect your child to work hard at school, expect your child to use manners, expect your child to get dressed on his or her own, expect your child to pray with you, expect your child to go to church, etc. With high frequency, your child will live up to whatever expectations you have for the child.

Parents who expect their child to act younger than his or her age create a child that is emotionally immature struggling in many areas of life. When a parent treats a child like a little boy or a little girl, the parent only hurts the child's development. Lowering expectations in such a manner creates a child that flounders year after year as an underachiever. Unfortunately, parents who view their child as younger than he or she is, unintentionally inhibit the maturity process making their child dependent on them for almost everything, even as adults.

Beginning at an early age, your goal is to expect your child to be responsible and exceed his or her chronological age in all aspects of life. Expect your child to act older than his or her age! Treating your child like he or she is two to three years older than his or her actual age will usually increase mature behavior.

Expect your child to respect peers and adults, expect your child to demonstrate politeness, expect your child to carry out chores, and expect your child to give a good consistent effort in life. When you see a successful, Godly life in your child's future, he or she will have that same picture in his or her mind.

Positive children have parents who expect that type of attitude. Those parents also believe the children will become responsible, successful adults. As a parent, continually picture your child with self-confidence and strong self-worth. Help your child dream big by believing in his or her talents and abilities. Expect the best for your child's future and he or she is highly likely to fulfill your visualization.

In terms of rules, clearly explain your ***expectations***. Often, when there is disobedience it comes from a parent not explaining the rules and not letting the child know what is expected of him or her. Children need to be told clearly what is expected in terms of acceptable and unacceptable behavior. As a parent, be proactive, not reactive, when it comes to setting boundaries to protect your child from harmful influences. Always evaluate how well you communicate what you *expect*.

In conclusion, please imagine your child as a reliable, confident, and successful adult. Then, *expect* that your child will make that picture a reality. Responsible children will one day become responsible adults, whereas irresponsible children are usually irresponsible adults. Responsible children also have parents who *expect* them to fulfill those expectations of being a capable, good decision-maker.

Make sure you have realistic goals and healthy expectations. For example, "My child will be a heart surgeon" is an unrealistic goal that neither the child nor the parent can control. However, "My child will pursue an education and give a good consistent academic effort" is a healthy expectation.

Your child will almost always fulfill the ***expectations*** you have for him or her. *Effective Parents* strongly desire their child to grow up so he or she will become a mature adult. Your ***expectations*** play a major role in keeping him or her on track toward life goals.

51. No Perfect Parent and No Perfect Child

Just as there are no perfect parents, there are also no perfect children. Romans 3:23 declares, "There is no difference, for all have sinned and fall short of the glory of God" (NIV). Every person is imperfect and flawed, yet many parents strive for perfection both in themselves and their children. Such high expectations produce continual personal disappointment and psychological issues. The effects of perfectionism can be devastating emotionally and behaviorally.

A perfectionistic parent is overly critical of others and his or her children. Such unhealthy parenting may cause a child to feel that imperfection equals failure, resulting in negative thoughts like "something is wrong with me." A child of a perfectionistic parent often compares himself or herself to other children, usually believing he or she never measures up.

A child who feels pressured to be perfect may experience anxiety, depression, anger, eating disorders, obsessive-compulsive disorder, control problems, and simply never feel good enough in life. Since a child is never able to attain the unattainable, he or she tends to just "give up" rather than keep trying.

Parents with perfectionistic expectations usually have very rigid and inflexible rules for their children. A perfectionistic parent possesses an excessive need for controlling nearly every aspect of the child's life from morning till bedtime. A child then becomes overly dependent on the parent living in constant fear of being inadequate and incompetent. A perfectionist parent holding unrealistic expectations may also cause the child to question if he or she is unconditionally loved.

It is normal to want your child to be the best in everything, but of course, that is unhealthy perfectionistic thinking. Perfection is the enemy of good! In the history of the world, a 100% obedient child has never existed. Through Jesus we are all forgiven for our imperfections.

Avoid perfectionism by welcoming your child's disobedience and daily missteps. Children learn best from their misbehavior, so view your child's mistakes as great learning opportunities. As a parent, you want your child to be imperfect, make mistakes, and be disobedient at times. Disobedience allows you to lead and guide your child toward responsible decision-making. Learning from his or her misbehavior and poor choices in the home, your child is likely to avoid major life mistakes as a teenager and adult.

As a parent, aim for realistic expectations as you train your child for *obedience*. Every day, relax and love your child unconditionally through the *Simple Habits* from Chapter Two while at the same time lovingly *applying the rules* found in Chapter Three.

52. Healthy Personal Life and Satisfying Marriage Equals Stability

The quality of your personal life will have a great deal to do with the quality of your parenting. Two healthy parents increase the probabilities of a responsible decision-making child, but it only takes one unhealthy parent to create an adult life full of struggles for a child.

An *Effective Parent* fully understands that for a child to enjoy each day, the parents' lives must be pleasing as well. When a parent does not have a pleasing personal life, the result is often dissatisfaction with life for a child.

Self-time is particularly important, so you must reserve recharge time for yourself on a regular basis. Since your child is an emotional sponge, your goal for personal happiness, contentment, and a positive attitude will be essential qualities your child needs to absorb from you.

Likewise, if you are married, the best thing you can do for your child is to love your spouse. It takes two to make a gratifying marriage, but only one to break the happiness connection. Most distressed marriages are the result of one spouse being unhealthy emotionally and/or behaviorally. Often, that unwholesome spouse is also a harmful parent who contributes to a child having various struggles.

Married couples who have frequent arguments may produce children with inner turmoil. Children raised by quarrelsome couples are also more likely to have negative adult relationships. Sadly, a high percentage of the time when there is a troubled child, there is also a troubled marriage. However, not all troubled marriages produce struggling or irresponsible children.

One of your primary responsibilities is to provide a loving home. A rewarding, happy marriage strongly increases the likelihood for a well-adjusted child. Your child is richly blessed when both of you are emotionally connected as a couple, as well as a united team in terms of parenting together. When parents are united in a gratifying marriage the child cannot play mom and dad against each other, creating a loyalty battle. Parents who are united as a happy couple have an easier process of establishing Biblical values within a child's character.

Having a rewarding marriage is also good role modeling for your child because he or she can observe the many words and behaviors that are vital for a satisfying relationship. If you are married, please consider reading ***Simple Habits for Marital Happiness: Practical Skills and Tools That Build A Strong Satisfying Relationship*** written by this author. When parents are loving with each other, they often consistently are nurturing with their children.

Every child needs both parents to be emotionally stable with rewarding individual lives. If you are married, one of the most important things you can do is work hard at continually improving and strengthening that relationship. A fulfilling *personal life* and, if applicable, a *solid marriage* foundation enables your child to develop into a reliable, capable adult.

CHAPTER 5

HABITS FOR A HAPPY, HEALTHY LIFE

Every child deserves to possess life skills like the ones explained in this chapter for a ***happy, healthy life***. The Bible declares, "Listen, my son, to your father's instruction and do not forsake your mother's teaching" (Proverbs 1:8 NIV). Schools, teachers, and churches are involved with the process, but most importantly, a parent will develop within a child the life skills that make a positive difference.

Look for teaching moments whether with social skills, manners, integrity, academic effort, money management, personal and domestic skills, etc.

A child learns from a parent's instruction, but these life skills must also be part of a parent's life. Be a life-long learner and use this knowledge to strengthen your present life skills and shore up weak areas.

Although learning life skills is an eighteen-year process for a child, begin today to instruct and exemplify how these *Simple Habits* are indispensable prerequisites for a successful, responsible adult life. Always be more focused on life skills that your child is learning versus day-to-day activities that are not essential in the long-term!

53. Optimism Creates a Positive Attitude

Being optimistic creates a positive attitude! Philippians 4:8 joyfully states, "Whatever is true, whatever is noble, whatever is right, whatever is pure, whatever is lovely, whatever is admirable—if anything is excellent or praiseworthy—think about such things" (Philippians 4:8 NIV).

That is positive thinking! With every challenge, stress the importance of positive self-talk which helps overcome fear.

Optimism is an important goal for every person to possess because that leads to a *positive attitude*. The home environment is what often produces an optimistic or pessimistic child. The good news is an *Effective Parent* can teach the skill of optimism to his or her child.

Pessimism originates from a helpless, hopeless feeling that nothing will ever change. Pessimistic parents are often critical, producing negative thoughts in a child's mind about himself or herself and the surroundings. A pessimist feels despondent that nothing in life matters because problems at home and school are not fixable. A pessimist feels problems are permanent rather than temporary, never going away, without any hope for improvement. If a child's mind is tattooed with pessimistic thinking, he or she starts experiencing negative results not only during childhood, but even worse in his or her future adult life.

An ***optimist*** accepts full responsibility when difficult times arise in life. An optimist perceives life's difficulties as temporary believing with every challenge comes solutions. An optimist trusts that every life trial comes to pass not to be long-lasting.

A ***Christian optimist*** is perpetually hopeful that, with God's help, he or she can overcome negative circumstances confidently believing every life issue has several solutions. Optimism is not false enthusiasm, but a thought process of treating challenges that happen almost daily in a positive way.

One of the best ways to influence a child is to model ***optimism*** starting at an exceedingly early age. As much as possible, only associate with other optimists and thankful people in your life. Assist your child in being a self-defense lawyer against negative thoughts by brainstorming with him or her solutions for obstacles and concerns.

Encourage the belief that, through prayer and God's grace, a person can cope with problems and handle any situation.

At a very early age, begin helping your child be a good finder with others and life circumstances, not a faultfinder. It is important for your child to recognize the blessings, accomplishments, or positives that occur each day in life. At the end of every day, an essential exercise is to ask your child to identify two successes or two joyful happenings he or she experienced.

Instill in your child positive thinking with a thankful heart and an appreciative attitude. Assist your child in recognizing all the little blessings in life. Talk regularly with your child about what is often taken for granted: a roof over his or her head, a bed in which to sleep, useful arms and legs, eyesight, hearing, food to eat, beautiful sunshine, freedoms, friendships, etc.

As an ***optimistic, positive*** parent, express encouragement and constant appreciation, which builds confidence and self-worth in your child. A healthy self-image then motivates your child to accomplish goals and tasks which helps eliminate "stinking thinking."

A parent can confidently change a child's life simply by becoming an ***optimist with a positive attitude***!

54. Learn Tremendously from Losing

I think of losing or failures as remarkably similar to stumbling and falling down. Every baby learning to walk stumbles, falls, and rises. The baby stumbles, falls, and rises over and over again until eventually he or she learns to walk. Any type of loss or failure in life that your child will experience is like a stumble. What is essential for your child is not the stumbling but the rising repeatedly because that leads to a life filled with determination.

Throughout life, your child will stumble in varying degrees on a regular basis. Stumbles may come from a poor grade on a test; an unfair action by a teacher or coach; bullying at school; a boyfriend/girlfriend breakup; an accident, etc. Your child will absolutely not be able to avoid daily stumbles, whether minor or major ones.

Unfortunately, too many parents will do almost everything possible to prevent their child from suffering a stumble. Some parents go to unbelievable extremes to be overprotective of their child. Overprotective parents live daily with the belief, "I need to protect 'my little baby' from stumbles of any kind. By continually holding my child's hand, I will ensure he or she has an enjoyable life."

I deeply appreciate the meaningful love such a parent possesses but that type of "protective care" will probably lead to tremendous problems for the child as an adult.

Starting at a young age, your child must learn how to handle losses or stumbles.

As a parent, you cannot be by your child's side for the rest of his or her life. The way your child reacts to adversity or failure is essential for success. It is unhealthy for a parent to coddle a child or, even worse, shield him or her from dealing with situations on his or her own. When your child fails, loses, or stumbles, encourage your child by assuring him or her you confidently believe the child can cope with the situation and rise again.

It is also detrimental for a parent to rarely provide opportunities for a child to encounter failures or setbacks. Introduce your child to activities that will allow your child to deal with losses and stumbles. Then, do not rescue him or her, but support the child in starting anew over and over.

Through activities and real-life experiences, teach your child that failures, losses, and stumbles are only events that do not define him or her as a person. Help your child learn from losses and stumbles, that he or she can and will rise over and over again. Teach your child to seek solutions with every life challenge.

A child must learn that losses and failures are never fatal, just as successes are never final. Instruct your child that valuable life lessons are learned from losses, stumbles, and setbacks. Develop within your child a growth mentality, so setbacks become springboards for future successes. As an *Effective Parent,* encourage, support, and help your child face losses and stumbles with confident abilities to cope and overcome life difficulties.

55. Provide Activities for Success

Successes definitely improve a child's self-confidence and self-esteem. A child develops optimism and a positive attitude from triumphs that occur through childhood experiences. Therefore, a parent needs to involve the child in a wide range of activities to provide many opportunities for continuous successes.

Of course, a child participating in various events will also experience failures, but those setbacks make whatever successes happen even sweeter. A major step in achieving success is failing, which creates a determination to never give up and persistently move toward the goal.

Too many parents focus their child's pursuits in just one specific area. When a child becomes a teenager, if that one activity does not work out, a child often feels like a failure. With no other interest or endeavor to achieve success, a teen may have lower self-worth, which often leads to poor decision-making and mischievous behavior.

The first eight years of my career, I was a high school educator. Four of those years, I was the assistant principal responsible for discipline when students misbehaved. What I discovered is that a teenager rarely got into trouble if he or she had even one area of success, which could be almost anything, good grades, sports, choir, science club, student government, student newspaper, yearbook, band, etc.

On the other hand, students sent to my office for discipline usually did not have even one accomplishment that enhanced their self-worth, giving them confidence in their overall abilities.

I will never forget one student who I thought had no successful activities, yet was a model citizen. He was always respectful to teachers, very polite, and never a problem. Although he was a below-average student and not involved in any school functions, he was an extremely nice Christian young man. One day when I had an opportunity to talk with him in private, I asked what he believed was one of his successes in life.

To my surprise he started talking about his love for roller skating. After a few "How" and "What" questions, I discovered he had tremendous success in roller skating competitions. For this outstanding Christian young man, roller skating was a solid success foundation that boosted his self-confidence and self-esteem, producing responsible decision-making in other aspects of his life.

Generate activities, events, or undertakings that can deliver triumphs for your child. Since you never know what may lead to areas of success, diversify your child's activities. It is also important to direct your child toward activities that are both beneficial and enjoyable for him or her. Success may come from sports like golf, tennis, swimming, bowling, volleyball, baseball, basketball, etc. Music experiences are easily available through band, choir, piano, guitar, etc. Other wonderful activities are scouting, drama, student government, dance, karate, chess, robotics, 4-H Club, etc.

Remember to also involve your child in some activities that can last into adulthood. Many adults are involved with golf, tennis, pickleball, bowling, and swimming well into their eighties. Singing in the high school choir or playing in the band may provide wonderful musical opportunities to praise the Lord in so many ways at church.

Expose your child to activities that may advance his or her career in the work environment. For example, a robotics or computer club can easily one day lead to a job in those fields. Many adults have told me playing golf as a youngster opened many doors in the business world just because they were somewhat skilled at golf.

If a child is never given the chance to participate in numerous activities, the child may never experience the valuable lessons of success and failure that are part of life. As an *Effective Parent*, make sure your child participates in a broad spectrum of activities, so that, as a teenager, he or she can narrow down the choices, selecting one or two that will help him or her build a positive, successful mindset.

56. Effort and Improvement are the Entire Focus

Every child needs to possess the internal truth that his or her parents believe in him or her. A child's perception of how the parent views him or her will often determine a child's success. For your child to have healthy self-esteem and feel encouraged, you need to continually praise your child's efforts with his or her special abilities and gifts.

One of the best ways an *Effective Parent* can instill confidence is through focusing on ***effort and improvement,*** not outcome and achievement. I believe it is extremely important for *Effective Parents* to frequently express how proud they are of their child's determination and effort, not their child's accomplishments. Complimenting *effort* and encouraging ongoing *improvement* creates positive energy within a child.

The parable of the talents (Matthew 25:14-30)—gifts or skills—illustrates what is important to Almighty God. The Bible says, "To one he gave five talents, to another, two, and to another, one, each according to his own ability" (AMP).

I am going to summarize the parable in my own words. The men receiving five and two talents doubled their talents and were told, "Well done, good and faithful servant" (Matthew 25:21). The man receiving one talent gave no effort, did not improve, still just had one talent, and was told "You wicked, lazy servant" (Matthew 25:26 NIV).

Almighty God focuses on a person's *effort and improvement* with gifts or skills so that should be the primary focus for an *Effective Parent*.

I do not want to hurt anyone's feelings, but I do not like bumper stickers that state, "My child is an honor student." The bumper sticker goes against the parable of the talents by focusing on achievement and accomplishment.

Let me explain with two fictitious children. Pam has an extremely high IQ, puts forth very little effort in school, but receives "As" and "Bs" because of her high intelligence and makes the honor roll. If Pam was motivated to use her significant intellectual abilities, she would probably earn straight "As" which is what God expects of her.

Patricia has a below-average IQ, works extremely hard by giving an excellent effort, but earns "Cs" and a few "Bs" not good enough for the honor roll. Which girl was a "good and faithful servant?" Of course, the answer is Patricia.

Not every child can earn good grades, make a sports team, or have a great voice to be in show choir. An *Effective Parent* takes the perspective of God by only being concerned about a child's *effort and improvement*. Value and show love to your child by never focusing just on outcome and successes, but on his or her growth and effort. Achievements and accomplishments build your child's self-worth, but every child has different talents and gifts that need to be complimented. You need to be proud of your child, and your child should feel internally proud, when he or she learns to fully use his or her gifts and skills daily, because that kind of ***effort and improvement*** pleases God.

57. Successful Social Skills

Due to our world of technology, what is often lacking for many children are *successful social skills* like using a person's name, making friends, greeting people, answering the phone, etc. A child who is socially competent will have a high probability of avoiding alcohol and drug abuse, not having a criminal record, and being able to resolve life challenges on his or her own. Successful social skills allow a child to easily relate to others in public situations and function well in society.

First and foremost, teach your child from an early age to frequently ***use a person's name*** when speaking to that person. Everyone likes to hear his or her name because that creates a feeling of importance. I am amazed how many adults rarely use a person's first name when conversing, yet, that is a critical social skill.

For example, "Olivia, how was your weekend?" "Olivia, what did you do for fun last night?" "Olivia, how long did it take you to finish your homework last night?"

If you re-read those questions aloud without speaking "Olivia," I hope you understand how impersonal that feels. For your child, an incredibly courteous social skill to learn is ***using a person's name*** when speaking with that person.

I have counseled hundreds of adults and children who are extremely anxious in social settings and at the same time struggle ***making friends***. Most people falsely believe that, to be likeable, one must be remarkably interesting by sharing wonderful news about what is going on in their life.

Individuals holding this false belief are often not self-centered, but mistakenly believe others will like them if they are interesting. Just the opposite is necessary for friendships. Your child and every person should not try to be interesting, but instead ***act interested in others***.

Being likeable comes through showing a genuine interest in another person's life, which creates an appealing factor for your child.

Hundreds of adults and children have learned to relax in public settings, as well as ***make friends*** through asking "How" and

"What" questions. When your child asks "How" and "What" questions of their peers, that creates feelings of acceptance, respect, and importance for that person.

For example, if your child met Mia for the first time at school and started asking questions like:

- "Mia, what is your favorite movie or TV show?"
- "Mia, how often do you ride your bicycle?"
- "Mia, what is your favorite fast-food restaurant?"
- "Mia, what do you like to do for fun at home?"

I can almost guarantee you Mia would believe your child is the nicest person in school.

With your child, role-play asking questions, so he or she is comfortable when opportunities arise. Role playing also assists your child in having a mental list of questions he or she might ask when around other children. As you read those questions, you may think it sounds interrogating, but it really is not because there will be a back-and-forth conversation. Asking "How" and "What" questions is a ***successful social skill*** that will relax your child, while giving him or her significant confidence in relationships.

Teach your child how to courteously introduce himself or herself when ***meeting someone for the first time***. Being comfortable initiating an introduction with someone new is a significant successful social skill.

The first ten seconds when meeting a person determines the quality of the connection. Teach your child to always greet others warmly with a smile, cheerful attitude, direct eye contact, standing tall, head held high, and extending a hand. Meeting someone for the first time usually involves a firm handshake that says, "I care about you," which means neither a "dead-fish" handshake nor an "iron-man" squeeze. Then, say something like, "Joe (use the person's name), so very nice to meet you. My name is

Sam." Or, "Joe, it is my pleasure to meet you, my name is Sam." Then your child should begin asking those open-ended "How" and "What" questions that value a person.

Never interrupt when the other person is speaking. When appropriate, compliment the other person. At the end of a conversation, your child should look that person directly in the eye with a large smile, shake hands, and say energetically something like, "Joe, it was so great to meet you. Have a very nice day!"

When ***making a phone call***, instruct your child to introduce himself or herself and then ask to speak with the person being called. Teach your child how to also ***answer the phone***. Recently, I spoke with a salesperson and the person greeted me with an unexcited, lackluster voice that broke my connection immediately. Great things in life are accomplished with enthusiasm. Have your child answer the phone with a cheerful, enthusiastic voice saying, "Good morning, this is Amelia."

Have your child treat others the way he or she wants to be treated!

As an *Effective Parent*, model these successful social skills of frequently using a person's name, making friends, greeting people for the first time, and answering the phone. Again, example is not the best teacher, example is the only teacher with your child. Be your child's ***social skills coach*** toward developing healthy relationships.

58. Magnificent Manners

Jesus said, "Love your neighbor as yourself" (Mark 12:31 NIV), which is demonstrated through respectful manners and courteous behaviors. As an *Effective Parent*, recognize your home is the school for learning manners, courtesy, and politeness when your child is in the public arena with others.

A child endowed with manners and courtesy is rarely self-centered, but instead focused on respecting, valuing, and serving others. An extremely important by-product for a child full of manners is also a stronger self-identity. When a child respects and values himself or herself and others, that will be naturally demonstrated in how he or she behaves. Manners and courtesy lead to mutual respect and politeness for relationships.

After counseling thousands of individuals, I have found that courtesy, politeness, and manners are extremely common in satisfying relationships but, sadly, noticeably absent in struggling, troubled relationships. Numerous homes would have a pleasant, relaxed atmosphere if family members would simply use manners, as well as courteous words and behaviors all the time.

Common courtesy has unfortunately become uncommon. A lack of manners, common courtesy, and mutual respect often leads to an absence of care and concern for people.

I truly believe that the utmost teaching of respect for others begins with using “sir” and “ma’am.” I was born and raised in Austin, Texas and nearly every child and adult regularly used “sir” and “ma’am” when addressing others. It seemed like each parent and teacher taught “sir” and “ma’am” as an essential expected courtesy, not an option. Beginning by three years of age, teach your child the importance of responding to adults with “Yes sir,” “No sir,” “Yes ma’am,” and “No ma’am” even if you live in a state where those manners are not believed to be essential.

Shown below are ten general guidelines that every child needs to possess as a responsible, respectful adult. Begin modeling and teaching these good manner principles at an early age.

1. Frequently use the words “please, thank you, you’re welcome.”
2. Saying “I am sorry” is important when appropriate.
3. Do not make fun of others and do not call names.
4. Hold the door, allowing others to enter a building as well as letting others off an elevator first.

5. After playing at another child's house, teach your child to express a "Thank you" both to the child and parents for being allowed to spend time at their home.
6. Cough or sneeze into one's elbow.
7. Say "Excuse me" when sneezing or accidentally bumping into another person.
8. When receiving any type of gift, say "Thank you" to that person. If you cannot thank the giver in person, send a written thank-you note. For a young child this can be a simple hand-drawn picture.
9. Whenever your child receives an invitation, let your child see you responding with a RSVP so he or she knows that it is always important to politely respond.
10. When someone asks, "How are you doing?" respond with a brief answer and ask the person in return, "And how are you doing?"

Per Lesson 18, table manners can only be taught when parents eat with their children. Demonstrating proper eating etiquette is important in life. There are seven basic table manners every person should possess.

1. Wait until everyone is seated and served before starting to eat.
2. Place a napkin in your lap before beginning to eat.
3. Use eating utensils in a proper fashion.
4. Ask for food items with a "Will you please pass . . ." rather than just reaching.
5. Never chew with your mouth open and don't talk with food in your mouth.
6. Express appreciation to the cook with "I appreciate . . ." or "Thank you . . ."
7. Always push your chair in when finished and take your plate, glass, and eating utensils to the kitchen sink.

A kind person usually has good manners, is courteous, and values others. Would most people say your child is a nice person? If you think yes, your child probably possesses manners and courtesies. As an *Effective Parent*, one of your main goals is to teach manners, courtesy, and proper etiquette because that produces a polite, kind, and respectful child.

59. Serving and Caring for Others

Jesus "came not to be served but to serve, and to give his life as a ransom for many" (Matthew 20:28 ESV). We are on this earth not to be served but to serve others. Hence, a child needs to understand the importance of *serving and caring for others.* 1 Thessalonians 5:11 instructs every person to "encourage *and* comfort one another and build up one another" (AMP). As an *Effective Parent*, you want your child to contribute in a meaningful way to society and others with a servant's heart like Jesus.

Developing Godly character comes in a variety of ways, so be intentional when creating that attitude. First and foremost, assist your child in becoming a tremendous helper around your home. Second, find opportunities for your child to contribute in various ways to the community. Finally, through conversing about world events, help your child learn to empathize with others experiencing losses.

Service starts in the home with helping in various ways. A child's self-worth is increased by supporting the smooth functioning of the home. Enhance your child's self-confidence through doing small tasks along with assisting other family members. Some examples of asking your child to help other family members are:

- Will you please help your sister with her math?
- Will you please get your brother his pacifier?
- Will you please find a band-aid for your mom's foot?
- Will you please read a story to your younger brother?

When it comes to contributing to society and serving others outside your home, you will probably need to work alongside your child. Contributing in meaningful ways to the community is "faith expressing itself through love" (Galatians 5:6 NIV), which empowers your child's Godly attitude. A child knowing how to love and serve people will make a difference in adult life. Shown below are some examples that may require you to be involved with your child.

- Support seniors from church by shoveling snow, mowing grass, etc.
- Help make and take a meal to a neighbor or friend in need.
- Your church may have volunteer activities so check what is available.
- Sponsor a child or a family at Christmas.
- Donate books to a women's shelter.
- Donate toys to Salvation Army or another local charity.
- Walk the neighbor's dog.
- Take flowers from your yard to a nursing home.
- Take treats to your local firehouse.
- Write thank-you cards to local police officers and take them to the police station.
- Serve food at a homeless shelter.
- Volunteer at the local food bank.

Empathy is an essential quality in *serving and caring for others*. When appropriate, one way to accomplish that objective is at times discuss losses that happen across the world due to tragic circumstances.

A word of caution . . . don't begin discussing heartbreaking events until the teenage years and ***be careful*** those conversations don't create sadness, anxiety, or depression within your teenager. Only discuss these distressing events on an irregular basis.

As I write this lesson, there are several heartbreaking examples:

- The world is experiencing a tragic pandemic. Briefly discuss how difficult it must feel to have the disease or for a loved one to die.
- Western states are battling horrible wildfires with loss of lives and homes. Discuss what it must *feel* like to lose a home from a fire.
- A couple of severe hurricanes have hit the gulf coast. Talk about how difficult it would be to have your home flooded.

Finally, pray with your child for those going through difficult times. Hebrews 10:24 summarizes this lesson through the exhortation, "Let us consider [thoughtfully] how we may encourage one another to love and to do good deeds" (AMP). As an *Effective Parent*, ***serving and caring for others*** is one more goal in leading your child toward adulthood.

60. Truthfulness, Honesty, and Integrity

Integrity is most often learned in childhood through parents who model that essential quality. The Bible states, "In everything set them an example by doing what is good. In your teaching show integrity, seriousness and soundness of speech that cannot be condemned" (Titus 2:7 NIV). One supreme value for a parent is unquestionable integrity.

Being a parent of integrity requires your outward match your inward. Integrity demands a parent always keep promises made to a child.

Truthfulness deals with spoken words while honesty involves moral actions. If your child views you being untruthful, he or she will also probably be untruthful. If your child sees you committing dishonest actions, he or she will also probably be dishonest.

When a parent fails to practice truthfulness and honesty, eventually that parent loses credibility in the eyes of the child.

Truthfulness and honesty are learned by a child from parents who model those qualities and require those behaviors from their child. Your child must witness you having truthful words and honest actions both in private and public. That means you also speak to family members and others in private the exact same way you speak to people in public. That behavior produces genuine integrity, which is truthfulness and honesty matching up.

Another way to heighten your integrity is by owning up to your mistakes. Acknowledging your wrongs and apologizing to your child only increases your integrity in your child's eyes.

Without integrity, it will be difficult for your child to trust you. Your child will believe in your integrity through what you say and do. And when your child sees your integrity, he or she will also have more confidence in your guidance.

An important goal is for your child to be truthful and honest because that establishes integrity. However, giving a consequence every time your child is untruthful may reinforce more untruthfulness, with the child covering up wrongdoings. Hence, do not always give a consequence or take away a privilege when your child is untruthful. When your child admits to being untruthful, give him or her a compliment with, "I am so very proud of you for being truthful" and then, at times, let it go.

As an *Effective Parent*, you must have consistent integrity which means your integrity should be present both in private and public. Always know that your child is an emotional sponge, so he or she will often demonstrate your personal truthfulness, honesty, and integrity.

61. Good Grooming

A lot of your child's self-image is based on his or her personal appearance. A child poorly dressed may be teased and ostracized by other children. On the positive side, a child "dressed for success" displays good grooming and healthy hygiene, which often leads to social acceptance. A positive overall neat appearance will cause your child to believe in himself or herself as well as provide credibility in the eyes of his or her peers. Feeling good about one's appearance will help produce the necessary self-assurance in order to cope with life challenges.

High school and college coaches have their players dress up on game days because they know their athletes will perform better when they feel good about their appearance. Athletic departments attempt to provide first-class locker rooms because having an attractive locker room enhances the players' self-worth, motivating them to perform at a higher level in the athletic arena.

In the seventies, I was a Lutheran high school teacher, and the school dress policy did not allow students to wear blue jeans. I realize today, jeans are a stylish statement for many young people, but at that time, jeans were viewed as casual, relaxed apparel. As a treat for the students, every so often they could wear jeans.

I found it interesting that almost every time a jeans day was permitted, the classroom discipline problems increased. I think it was probably due to students believing that, with less formal dress, they could unwind, let loose, and not listen as well to their teachers.

The state of dress often reflects the mental health of a person. After counseling thousands of individuals, I find it interesting that anxious and depressed adults and children are often not concerned about their appearance and grooming. They sometimes do not bathe, brush their teeth daily, care if they have body odor, and will wear wrinkled or dirty clothes.

On the other hand, I discovered individuals who are responsible and successful at life are focused on how they look to others, which enhances their self-worth and self-confidence. A child can be dressed nicely and be confident with his or her appearance even if the clothes were purchased at a thrift store.

Some parents think they can wait until the teen years to encourage their child to be concerned about physical appearance but that is simply too late. It is particularly important to begin by even three years of age with good grooming habits, dressing neatly, and taking pride in one's appearance.

When your child looks good, your child feels good. And when your child feels good, he or she has more confidence in handling life's responsibilities. Within the family budget, a parent should purchase clothes and shoes that fit well and look nice to build a child's self-esteem. Always have the child wear clean, unwrinkled clothing with shoes that are not dirty.

Daily hygiene is something your child needs to learn through your encouragement. Cleanliness with no body odor is critical to self-respect. As your child becomes older, teach him or her to bathe daily and always use deodorant. For boys, hair should be combed and facial hair well-groomed. For girls, hair should be clean and styled. Being well-groomed on a daily basis also means brushing teeth at least twice a day and flossing once a day.

I have happily heard hundreds of times a parent share something like, "I am amazed how daily bathing, nice clothes, or sharp tennis shoes improved my child's attitude and even lifted his or her depression." Parents have also shared how assisting their child in organizing the bedroom produced improved academic effort at school.

A parent must set the example by practicing care for personal dress and hygiene. An *Effective Parent* wants the child to feel respect for himself or herself, so have your child implement beneficial grooming habits. Maintaining and enjoying a healthy physical appearance boosts self-image, which increases a child's probabilities for success with others, school, and life.

62. Time Management and Organization Skills

Ecclesiastes 3:1 declares, "There is a time for everything" (NIV), including time management and organization skills. A wise adult who is a Godly steward of his or her time usually learned that significant skill as a child. The goal with ***time management*** and ***organization skills*** is establishing good habits for a lifetime. It is difficult to be successful at one's endeavors without knowing how to effectively manage time and organize one's life. This lesson is more focused on older children but can be simplified to benefit younger ones as well.

A productive, successful person lives on purpose with a plan for scheduling the day. Time management is simply staying in charge of one's day, so the various activities do not control your child. Your child does not need to be so specific that he or she schedules each hour of the day. Children need to be children and a flexible schedule allows that to happen.

Time management and ***organization skills*** help your child prioritize what is most important for every day, a significant quality of adult achievers. Time management also establishes better balance in life for your child. Gently teach your child to be deliberate in how he or she schedules time with homework, play time, family time, etc.

Beginning at kindergarten, teach your child the value of *time management* and the importance of organizing his or her daily and weekly schedule. Some parents, and even schools, have a planning book so a child can organize and visualize the entire day. Every Sunday, sit down with your child and discuss the week's schedule. Then, each evening of that week, review the next day. Perhaps ask, "What are your two most important goals for tomorrow?"

Keep in mind that while scheduling can be advantageous, over-scheduling can be detrimental to a child's health and the family's happiness.

Capable children are not only good time managers but also organized. As an *Effective Parent*, teach your child how to organize his or her surroundings. Communicate that everything has a place, so after using any item put it back in that same spot.

Organizing clothes, school supplies, toys, etc. can save your child a lot of time simply because he or she does not have to search for things.

A messy, disorganized living environment often leads to lower self-worth and a chaotic internal feeling for a child. Your home and car need to be orderly and have an acceptable appearance. As a parent, whether you live in an apartment or a house, have an older car or a new automobile make sure that your home and car are decluttered and organized.

Each evening have your child take five minutes to straighten the bedroom to create calmness for the next morning. During the school year, organizing the night before can set your child up for a successful school day. Perhaps assist your child in determining what clothes will be worn the next day, pack the book bag for school, prepare lunch boxes, etc.

At night, review with your child a short mental list of responsibilities for the next day to establish a plan, thus, creating a peaceful sleep. However, do not let that mental list produce stress for your child.

Every child wants to make choices for himself or herself. *Time management* and *organization skills* assist with making responsible decisions. Time management and organization skills also enhance your child's self-discipline and self-motivation. A child who views himself or herself as competent at ***time management*** and ***organization skills*** will usually perceive himself or herself as a capable, successful person in nearly all aspects of life.

63. Personal and Domestic Skills

Benjamin Franklin said, "By failing to prepare, you are preparing to fail." That wise statement applies to a parent who doesn't prepare a child with numerous personal and domestic skills. The sooner a child achieves the skills that follow in this lesson, the more likely he or she will be a competent, dependable, and responsible adult.

Please remember to expect your child to act older than his or her age. Treating your child like he or she is two to three years older than the child is, will usually increase mature behavior, including acquiring skills sooner than later in life.

Although not comprehensive, the following are suggested skills that will benefit children before graduating from high school. Again, each skill is dependent on a child's age and maturity level.

Personal Skills

Dress, undress themselves	Brush teeth
Wash face	Comb hair
Tie shoes	Bathe unsupervised
Memorize home address	Sit quietly in church
Make an emergency call	Memorize parents' cell phone number
Cross the street safely	Feed and water pets
Stay home alone	Clean bathroom sink, toilet, and tub
Use a computer	Arrange for haircuts

Belongings

Put toys away	Plan clothes for the next day
Make own bed	Straighten up bedroom and bathroom
Organize drawers and closet	Place dirty clothes in hamper
Fold clothes	Help with own laundry
Change own bed sheets	Use washing machine and dryer

Household Skills

Empty waste baskets	Dust
Use broom and dustpan	Use a vacuum cleaner
Wash windows	Replace light bulbs
Mop floor	Simple mending

Cooking Skills

Make a sandwich	Pack a lunch
Make a tossed salad	Make scrambled eggs
Prepare boxed macaroni and cheese	Cook frozen vegetables
Follow recipe directions	Bake cookies and a cake
Make pancakes and waffles	Grill burgers and hot dogs
Plan and shop for balanced meals	Cook an entire dinner

Outdoor Skills

Ride a bike	Rake leaves
Weed garden	Water flowers and garden
Mow lawn and edge drive	Trim shrubs
Shovel snow	Wash the car

Money Skills

Identify money denominations	Count and make change
Make a bank deposit and withdrawal	Write a check
Balance a checkbook	Use a credit card
Compare prices when shopping	Return an item to a store properly

Kitchen Skills

Set table	Clear table
Load and turn on dishwasher	Empty dishwasher
Clean stove	Put away groceries

Automobile Skills

Drive a car	Fill car with gas
Fill tires with air	Clean interior of the car
Check oil	Drive on an interstate
Take a taxi or car for hire	Be able to utilize GPS

Other Skills

Understand proper use of medicines	Be able to swim
Learn emergency first aid	Babysit younger siblings or children
Change filter in furnace	Do simple home repairs

Parenting without goals is like shooting without a target. Almost every *Effective Parent* has goals for his or her child, including personal and domestic skills, to help guide the child toward a successful life. Have a clear plan for moving your child in the direction of these valuable life proficiencies.

Incrementally, learning these skills can also have a profound effect on your child's self-motivation and self-confidence. The quality of your child's future life will have a great deal to do with the quantity and quality of personal and domestic skills learned in childhood.

64. Household Chores

Chores are a reality of life because every person has daily chores. A chore is defined as any routine job around the house needed for the smooth functioning of the home, many of which are listed as life skills. Chores teach a child how to work, an absolutely essential life skill. Doing regular chores is a significant quality to cultivate in a child because that often results in a happy adult life.

Proverbs 16:3 states, "Commit your work to the Lord, and your plans will be established" (ESV). Consistency with chores creates a child who is self-disciplined and often has a great work ethic.

Household chores are early preparation for the workforce, being an adult, marriage, and perhaps parenthood. When a child begins completing household duties, that promotes a feeling of responsibility and competency upon which he or she can build a strong foundational future. Every time a child accomplishes a chore, that increases the internal belief that he or she is capable of also succeeding at life. Hence, completing chores infuses a child with self-confidence boosting his or her self-esteem.

The popular adage is true, "There is no such thing as a free lunch." When a child is physically able, begin with chores *as early as three or four years of age* so he or she starts to internalize the wisdom in that saying. Doing chores at an early age also increases the probabilities for a child to be an effective employee and perhaps entrepreneur one day.

The purpose of a chore is to develop responsibility, self-discipline, and self-worth.

Jesus came "to serve" (Matthew 20:28) and a child carrying out tasks becomes an effective helper and worker. Developing this strong work ethic then fosters the mindset for a child, "I am a hard worker."

The benefits of regular household chores are priceless because the more chores a child can master, the quicker he or she begins making mature, responsible decisions. Doing chores helps a child feel competent which instills a sense of responsibility and self-pride cultivating the encouraging belief that he or she is growing up. Healthy self-esteem occurs within a child when he or she accomplishes tasks increasing the internal conviction that he or she can succeed at life. Chores also provide opportunities for planning and time management. Remember to utilize "When you/Then you" with household chores to develop self-reliance, discipline, and motivation that work must be done before play can be enjoyed.

When a child completes a chore, it is another opportunity for a parent to give an *Appreciation Vitamin*. Positive labels are especially important so after accomplishing a task a parent can easily say, "*I appreciate* you being a great *helper or worker*." Adults who are happy learn early in life to "do their way to happiness," which is a tremendous benefit for a child completing chores.

An overprotective parent may hesitate to give chores to a child which hurts a child's maturity level and lowers his or her self-esteem. An unproductive child often ends up feeling useless and helpless.

Have a consistent schedule with chores because a child benefits from knowing what a parent expects. A whiteboard chore chart may help a child visualize and understand what needs to be accomplished each day.

During the week, limit the length of time for chores. Sports, homework, and other activities do not diminish chore responsibilities, but the tasks given should take less time for a child involved in activities. Sadly, some parents go overboard with too many chores or too lengthy ones, which will negatively impact a child's emotional well-being and may cause rebellion.

An important point to remember is, a parent will almost always complete chores better and faster than a child. How well the job is done is not the priority.

I counseled a high school student who was failing academically and extensively using drugs. Throughout his life, his parents had not given him chores because they could do the tasks "better than their son." Both parents were perfectionistic, and I remember the dad saying his son "misses strips of grass when he mows the lawn, totally unacceptable so I don't let him mow."The son's self-esteem was at the bottom of the barrel. Having the cleanest bathroom or best mown yard is not the goal!

Saturdays are usually a good day for all family members to do household chores together. A child then learns he or she is a critical part of the family. Not only can tasks be done in less time, but a stronger emotional connection will also be established with family members. Working side by side, a child observes a parent setting the example of hard work along with functioning together to make a valuable contribution toward successful family living.

Having a child do chores is probably one of the best ways to raise a successful, responsible child and may be considered one of the greatest parenting strategies. A wise, *Effective Parent* creates continual practice with household chores to develop initiative, self-confidence, and high self-worth.

65. Money Management Through an Allowance

The goal with an allowance is to help a child understand finances and how to handle money in a responsible, Godly fashion. When it comes to teaching a healthy perspective of money, a parent's spending habits will speak volumes about either "laying up treasures" on earth or being "rich toward God" (Luke 12:21 ESV).

A child who views a parent as excessively concerned with possessions or expensive activities often experiences spiritual harm. A parent focused on purchasing things will never be satisfied because constantly acquiring material things leads to wanting more and more—one will simply never be content.

The magnet of excessive materialism blocks a child's view of the importance for what Jesus said, "Be on your guard against all kinds of greed" (NIV Luke 12:15). A parent's actions in terms of spending money speak so loudly the child cannot hear what they are saying, because seeing is what truly creates the life lesson of handling money. A parent setting a responsible example, along with an allowance properly given, can assist a child to develop money management skills to be "rich toward God" (Luke 12:21 ESV).

Guidelines on handling an allowance are plentiful and varied. There is no one correct design for allowances that applies to every family. Nonetheless, establish a plan for expectations to be clear regarding the allowance system. First, determine a specific day for giving your child the allowance. Second, be consistent with the same amount of money each week.

A common practice is for a child to divide the allowance into ***giving***, ***saving***, and ***spending*** in that priority order. The suggested percentages for each are: ***giving*** = 10%: ***saving*** = 10-20%; and ***spending*** = 70-80%. Discuss and explain the reasons for having three categories and placing *giving* and *saving* ahead of *spending.*

When discussing *giving,* emphasize that the money is an *offering to the Lord* whether it is given to a church or charity. To say "*give* to church" does not convey the true meaning of an *offering to God* for a child or even an adult. A *savings* account should continually increase and not just be used for pleasure purchases that can wipe out the savings account eventually. A healthy parental statement regarding *spending* is, "I want to guide your spending practices. You can spend your allowance on what you want under my supervision."

Start providing an allowance around the age of five. The amount for an allowance will often depend on the family income. A general rule of thumb is to give an allowance that ranges from $0.50 to $2 per week for each year of a child's age up to the age of thirteen. For example, if the amount is one dollar, a nine-year-old child would receive nine dollars per week.

For teenagers, an allowance is dependent on what it covers. I suggest an allowance to pay for enjoyable activities and not necessary expenditures like clothing, gas, car insurance, etc. Teens may also be given a higher allowance ranging from $2 to $5 per week for each year of age depending on a teen's expenditures and the family income. Beginning about the age of thirteen, a teenager should be encouraged to earn spending money by mowing lawns in the neighborhood, babysitting, etc. Eventually, a part-time job can make a big difference for a teen seeking more discretionary spending funds.

Using money as a reward for good grades, nice behavior, or completing tasks rather than praise is simply not a healthy idea. Never connect an allowance to a chore or task. Hence, children should not be paid for doing particular chores around the house. Paying a child for doing specific chores in order to earn an allowance only lowers a child's self-esteem. Hard work associated with doing chores overcomes the feeling of entitlement by parents doing everything for him or her.

Children should contribute toward home maintenance by doing chores. Everyone in the home shares both the work and a portion of the family income. Serving the family by being a worthy helper produces a good feeling which can never be achieved through a financial reward.

However, a child can be paid for doing something that a parent would normally hire someone else to do. For example, if a parent would take the automobile through a car wash for a cost of $10, a teen could wash his or her parent's car for $10. Or if a parent would pay a person to paint the front door for $50, then the teen could paint the front door for $50. Or if a parent planned to pay a lawn service $30 per week, a teen could mow the grass and edge the driveway to receive that $30.

An adult may borrow money for a house or car, but it is not a good idea to borrow for extravagant items. Likewise, almost never give an advance on an allowance because that is borrowing money for gratification, usually due to poor budgeting. Children need to learn that, when the spending portion of their allowance is gone, it is gone.

Another way to teach money management is to give your child a lunch allowance. Ensure that the amount is sufficient, so your child does not go hungry at lunch. I have witnessed parents giving inadequate funds for lunch and the child is out of money after Wednesday or Thursday. A parent then blames the child, when, in fact, it is the parent's mistake for giving the child insufficient lunch funds. A lunch allowance is a great idea for teaching a child how to handle cash and make it last for an entire week.

An allowance provides a parent with an opportunity to teach *giving to God*, *saving*, and *spending* money skills. ***Money management through an allowance*** is an important life lesson that every child must learn.

66. Two Adult Milestones for a Teenager

Rarely will a young adult child have difficulty becoming independent and leaving home when he or she ***learns to drive*** at the legal age and has a ***part-time job*** before graduating high school. Sadly, I have counseled many adults who never attained either one of these objectives in high school. The result was they often struggled being capable, competent adults because they lacked confidence.

Please realize that, if you live where cars are not a viable option, but subways and trains are, then learning to drive may not be a goal. Please also understand that a part-time job in the workplace may not always be feasible, but regular babysitting, mowing lawns, washing cars, etc. may be an alternative.

Driving is one of the first steps toward becoming an independent adult. Being able to drive a car can help a teen's maturity level and build responsibility. Leaving home in a car provides a certain amount of freedom that is also a stepping-stone toward adulthood. A sixteen-year-old driver often de-stresses a parent and the home environment by being able to drive to school, job, personal activities, and run errands.

A parent teaching a child to drive can enhance the parent-teen relationship. While sitting in the passenger seat, a parent can provide positive communication through constant encouragement and numerous compliments. Practice driving affords automatic parent-teen time together and even an enjoyable treat afterwards to further connect. One other benefit, losing the privilege of driving a car, is a tremendous incentive for a teen to complete schoolwork, be respectful, and finish chores.

Please understand that some teens will not have the maturity or decision-making skills to drive a car at sixteen. When you have a teenager, assess his or her decision-making in terms of an understanding for risks and rewards with a fast vehicle. A realistic question is, "Can my sixteen-year-old handle the responsibility of life and death decisions with a 3,000-pound automobile?"

Certainly, there are significant dangers associated with a sixteen-year-old driving a car because that is a leading cause of death and disabilities for young people. Also be prepared for some fender benders because that happens for a percentage of teens.

If a teenager can obtain a driver's license, an *Effective Parent* should establish rules and expectations for using a car. A sixteen-year-old earns the privilege to drive through responsible decisions and adhering to safety rules like always wearing a seat belt. Other crucial expectations to share are that reckless driving will never be tolerated just as alcohol use with a car is an absolute NO.

There are some other considerations to keep in mind. Teens are sometimes sleep deprived. The effects of sleep deprivation on driving are absolutely shocking. The risk of crashing a car increases dramatically for drivers who are sleep deprived. Teens with attention deficit disorder (ADD) are also at greater risk and need to take their medication appropriately. Another key question is, "How responsible are a teen's peers when driving a car?" Many teenagers drive in a similar fashion to their friends.

A teenage driver produces an additional expense with the cost of insurance, gas, and perhaps even another car. That financial cost can be offset by the teenager having a part-time job. Both milestones are achieved when a teen has a driver's license and can drive to the job.

For a teenager, a ***part-time job*** is preparation for full-time employment in only a few years. The benefits of part-time work are a healthy transition to adulthood, a sense of responsibility, learning to be a positive team member, key customer service skills, increased independence, and lessons in personal finance like saving for the future. An *Effective Parent* can partner with his or her teenager in achieving this second milestone which can be a positive, rewarding experience. When a child is involved in after-school activities, part-time work may happen during the summer months.

Online, there are examples of one-page resumes. Working with his or her parent can help a teenager with the challenge of writing and formatting a resume. Besides a resume, things to consider when searching for a part-time job are: list of places to apply, preparation for an interview, good grooming, social skills, and confident communication skills.

When possible, begin the process by helping your teen network with family contacts, neighbors, teachers, pastors, and even other peers who have a part-time job. It helps to have another person recommend a teen to an employer. Consider what a potential job offers, that is, fun, great work experience, learning a new skill, etc. Begin by making a long list of possibilities, then trim down the list through a pros and cons process.

Think outside the box with a list of employment places. For example, I counseled some teens who worked at a golf course, cleaning golf carts, and then recharging them for the next day. Besides having part-time work at the course and handling golf carts, these teens enhanced their driving skills as well.

Finally, keep in mind that a teenager's full-time job is giving a good consistent effort in high school. Research has found though that a teen's grades are actually better when involved with school activities or a part-time job. The reason: A student must manage time well in order to be successful at school and the activity or job. Ideally, a teenager should never work more than twelve to fifteen hours per week during the school year.

Achieving these two milestones in high school is critical in preparing a child for successful adulthood. Having a ***driver's license*** and a ***part-time job*** assists a teenager in gaining independence while increasing responsible decision-making, which is a major life goal. Attaining these two adult tasks also improve self-motivation, self-confidence, and self-image. When your child has accomplished both critical objectives before graduating high school, you can feel more confident that your child will be a capable, responsible adult.

67. Sports Involvement

An *Effective Parent* involves a child in activities (see Lesson 55) and sports that teach self-discipline, self-confidence, how to handle setbacks, and enhance character qualities. Athletic activities accomplish those four objectives and even more. Being involved together in a sports activity also enables a parent to enjoy more bonding time with his or her child. Sports are positive in so many ways, prevalent in societies around the world, and often a major part of leisure discussions at work.

Having been both a high school head varsity football coach and basketball coach, I have seen firsthand the benefits of involving a child in sports. Truly tremendous life lessons are learned from athletic involvement. Sports teach a child how to:

- Be a humble winner by not boasting.
- Be a gracious loser by congratulating the winner.
- Develop a supportive teamwork attitude.
- Stay strong when things are not going well.
- Have a respectful attitude toward the adults providing instruction, opponents, and referees.

I believe athletic involvement has numerous similarities to ongoing life experiences for a child. Sports teach a child to live in the moment and forget the past. Sports teach a child to stay positive and believe in himself or herself even in the face of adversity! Sports teach a child to say, "I can and I will focus on the next golf swing, volleyball hit, free throw, pitch, etc." Sports enable a child to speak with conviction, "I will always be determined and *never, never, never give up*!" Sports build an internal strength to be mentally tough and stay strong through every life hardship.

When a child participates in a sports activity, he or she is automatically introduced to losses, a consistent occurrence in adulthood. One of the best reasons for engaging a child in athletics is affording him or her the learning opportunity for how to handle losing mentally and emotionally. In baseball, strikeouts happen, home runs are hit off a pitcher, and knees are bloodied from a hard slide. In golf, the ball ends up deep in the woods or, even worse, the water leading to bogeys, double bogeys and even triple bogeys, and the wind can make for a horrible round of golf.

In volleyball, swimming, cross-country, basketball, soccer, tennis, track, lacrosse, football, hockey, etc., there are equally tough times and setbacks. And your child may not make the team, which is like not getting a job after an interview. Yet, all these losses and difficult experiences will only benefit a child as an adult, when he or she experiences various obstacles.

Regularly practicing sports easily inserts exercise into a daily routine. A physically fit child is often more emotionally stable, self-confident, relaxed, and able to give a good consistent effort academically. A child who is physically unfit is more inclined to struggle with self-motivation, self-confidence, academic challenges, and social relationships with others.

Many individuals will not participate in high school sports primarily due to the highly competitive selection factor. Nonetheless, there are numerous opportunities for youth sports involvement from the ages of four to eighteen. An active lifestyle and positive experiences are foundational with athletic involvement.

Sports have numerous benefits for a child by improving self-esteem, physical health, teamwork, leadership abilities, social skills, energy levels, mental health, and discipline. Your child's quality of life can be easily enhanced through recreational sports that often transition to physical activity in adulthood.

CHAPTER 6

HABITS THAT PREPARE A CHILD FOR THE WORLD

One of the most demanding tasks that a parent faces today is preparing a child to live in a sinful world that seems to move more and more away from God with each passing day. The Bible encourages every believer, including your child, to live a Godly life by avoiding "wicked" associations and finding delight in God's Word. "Oh, the joys of those who do not follow the advice of the wicked, or stand around with sinners, or join in with mockers. But they delight in the law of the Lord, meditating on it day and night" (Psalms 1:1-2 NLT). Due to diminishing Biblical values, and a self-centered, pleasure-seeking society, a child needs exceptional knowledge, skills, and parental guidance to be faithful in his or her Christian walk.

This chapter contains essential wisdom that makes a significant difference for enhancing a child's confidence to establish healthy life habits, overcome obstacles, and avoid temptations. As an *Effective Parent*, utilize the valuable information in these eighteen lessons to equip your child with practical skills and knowledge to cope effectively with this sinful world. Helping your child learn to deal with life challenges is a tremendous task, but through the commonsense solutions found in this chapter, you can support your child in handling potential life stressors to lead a Godly life.

68. Morning and Bedtime Routines

Two of the most important routines are morning and bedtime. When mornings are pleasant and encouraging, then probabilities are good the day will be positive for your child. Likewise, when bedtime goes well for your child, then sleep will most likely be sound. Consistency with both routines helps a parent overcome frustration and parent-child conflicts. The following suggestions are ideal routines that are at least good targets at which to take aim.

In terms of a ***morning routine***, studies have found that your child's first five minutes need to be positive because that often establishes his or her attitude for the entire day. Hence, the entire morning, strive to avoid the "Cs" of correction, criticism, complaining, and condemnation, especially the first five minutes.

A successful child generally has a schedule to follow every morning before school. One healthy guideline is no TV, computer, tablet, or other technology gadgets because that distracts from the main goal of the morning, preparing for school.

A full breakfast is beneficial because research has found that a good breakfast enables a child to do better in school. A breakfast routine of a specific breakfast for each day of the week can de-stress a parent and provide stability for a child. Eating breakfast together may be difficult for some families, but whenever possible, do it for the uplifting parent-child conversation.

Sadly, I have had children tell me their parents don't get up with them in the morning. Those children are often anxious, depressed, and poor students. When possible, a parent needs to be present with the child during the entire morning routine. Remember also to give your child a big hug goodbye and tell him or her, "I love you no matter what! Have a great day!"

A ***bedtime routine*** is an invaluable life habit for your child that can carry over into adulthood. Generally, a consistent pre-bedtime routine should begin well before your child's target time to fall asleep. Having a bedtime routine lets your child's body know sleep is just around the corner. A consistent routine also relaxes a child and leads to falling asleep quicker.

Usually set a limit with no caffeine and sugar after 7:00 p.m. It is also a good idea to not have any electronic devices in the bedroom. I have counseled hundreds of young people who were regularly sleep deprived because of having a cell phone, tablet, or laptop next to their bed that they used throughout the night.

Allow adequate time before bedtime to review the next day's activities including schoolwork. Perhaps ask, "What are special goals or tasks to be achieved the next day?" If some responsibilities are unfinished, allow some time to complete those responsibilities if possible.

On school nights, approximately one hour before bedtime, turn off the television, computer, and tablet. Perhaps have your child read a book or a Bible story with you. Prevent rushing your child by allowing enough time for changing into pajamas, brushing teeth, and using the bathroom. On weekends, TV, computer, and tablet time can be a special privilege up until bedtime.

Teenagers need to make many of their own decisions. Nonetheless, on school nights when a teen learns to go without technology approximately one hour before falling asleep, he or she develops a good habit.

Bedtime preparation can actually make the morning routine much smoother. Discuss the next day's weather and decide upon clothes to wear, perhaps even setting them out to save time the next morning. Loading the school backpack during this time can help the morning go smoother.

Develop a bedtime tuck-in routine for your child. Always ensure that tuck-in time is a positive experience. An encouraging conclusion to the day before lights out can be very calming and reassuring for your child. Discussing stressful events may make bedtime difficult. Perhaps say a prayer with your child at bedside. Before you leave the bedroom, reassure your child with, "I will love you even more tomorrow than I did today!" (Lesson 14).

I just described the perfect ***morning*** and ***bedtime routines,*** which may not happen every day but are worthy targets. Planning often is the difference between a successful night's sleep and a positive beginning to a new day for your child versus the opposite. If some of these ideas do not work for you, then come up with your own morning and bedtime routines, but ***have a plan for your child's sake***!

69. Sleep Is Significant

Sufficient sleep is significant for every person, including your child. Sleep has a profound impact on your child's physical health, emotional well-being, and mental stability. An appropriate amount of sleep improves your child's thinking abilities. Sound sleep simply enhances your child's overall well-being and may improve academic performance. Sleep is just as important as a balanced diet and a good breakfast.

Whenever an adult or child attends counseling, one of my initial goals is to assess the quantity and quality of the sleep. After counseling numerous individuals, I found that, for many counselees, sleep may be at the heart of their life struggles.

An irregular sleep schedule throws off your child's biological clock. Sleep deprivation can cause your child to struggle with a lack of confidence, irritability, and mood swings. An ongoing lack of sleep may also produce anxiety and depression within your child.

A sleep-deprived child may feel like he or she is in a "fog" from fatigue. Insufficient sleep will cause your child's cognitive ability to drop, leading to impaired judgment. Without enough sleep, a child often makes poorer decisions, is more impulsive, and makes riskier choices. Insufficient sleep cripple's memory and concentration making it difficult for your child to learn. Academically, inadequate sleep limits your child's brain health, which affects school performance.

Years ago, parents brought their ten-year old daughter for counseling to help with her anxiety, depression, and poor school functioning. Since the age of four, this girl had these three issues and even more problems. For six years, the daughter had counseled with other psychologists, been evaluated for ADD, as well as learning disabilities. The results were all negative. Sadly, nothing helped, and this girl's problems continued.

I began by asking the parents about their daughter's sleep schedule along with the quality of her sleep. The parents reported their daughter rarely fell asleep at the same time each night and frequently woke up during the night, almost never sleeping through the night.

I suggested the parents purchase a vitamin sleep supplement and begin giving that to her thirty minutes before bedtime. The results were amazing! She started experiencing a sound, full night of restful sleep, which turned her life around—having an easier time with homework, better school performance, and even more friends. Certainly, sleep is not a "magical cure" for all life problems, but it does help a lot.

An essential goal for your child is adequate sleep every night!

Have a consistent time for your child to fall asleep and then wake up at approximately the same time to keep the internal body clock on schedule. Help your child learn that maintaining a regular sleep schedule often improves his or her overall well-being. Shown below are seven specific suggestions for more restful sleep.

1. Your child needs to slow down before he or she eventually stops. Prepare for sleep by spending enough time in calm, relaxing activities.

2. One hour before bedtime, avoid bright images and loud noises because that is mentally stimulating on a subconscious level.
3. Have your child read before bedtime, which causes the eyes to have a back-and-forth horizontal movement triggering the brain to sleep.
4. Avoid naps after 3:00 p.m. A nap after school makes it difficult for your child to fall asleep, leading to a vicious cycle of staying up late, being tired all day with poor mental concentration, and then taking a nap the next day after 3:00 p.m.
5. Keep your child's bedroom cool and dark. Too much light in the bedroom makes it difficult for a restful sleep.
6. No TV or music when the lights are out. A quiet bedroom helps your child fall asleep.
7. Consider using a lavender scented oil or lotion to help with sleep.

The average amount of sleep needed varies from person to person. Generally speaking, a child from the ages of five to nine should aim for ten to eleven hours of sleep; for ten to twelve years of age, a good goal is nine to ten hours; and for thirteen to eighteen, a sleep target of eight to nine hours is ideal. Please check with your child's medical doctor to get a professional opinion.

Your child's mind and body demand adequate sleep. It is imperative that your child gets enough sleep on a regular basis. As an *Effective Parent*, do whatever it takes to develop sound sleep habits for your child.

70. Consistent Academic Effort

My definition of ***consistent academic effort*** is *not the grades achieved*, but a child giving an "A-" for effort in every class!

Reading and *math* are of supreme importance in terms of predicting how well your child does academically, as well as an adult. That is why math and reading are two skills that must be mastered by your child!

There are significant factors that lead to a higher intellect and academic success. First, in order to develop your child's intellectual capability, from six months to two years, spend hours upon hours reading to your child and conversing with him or her. Those eighteen months will significantly influence your child's intellectual quotient. This must continue through early childhood because that is tremendously beneficial for his or her academic development.

Develop your child's math skills by asking him or her to solve general math problems in your life like simple addition and subtraction. If you are able financially, purchase computer programs that teach reading and math skills as early as preschool age. Have plenty of books and reading materials in your home.

Another important factor for a healthy life is social skills. Frequent interaction with your child on a daily basis is absolutely indispensable. Remember the importance of social skills (see Lesson 57) to increase confidence in speaking with peers and when necessary approaching the teacher with questions.

Parents of motivated students provide stimulating educational activities for their child like board games and computer games. An *Effective Parent* will also offer many opportunities for success in various aspects of life (see Lessons 55 and 67) to build confidence for improved *academic effort*. A parent of an achiever never uses money as a reward for grades, but instead focuses on praise along with encouragement for *effort* and *improvement*.

Competent students begin school *only when they are ready*, not necessarily when they reach the correct chronological age. Generally speaking, boys are approximately six months behind girls in terms of maturity. Hence, it is wise to allow a son to be older for his grade in order to ensure he is ready for school. I have never witnessed one boy who was hurt emotionally or embarrassed when he was somewhat older before beginning school.

An extremely important skill for your child to acquire is learning to memorize for quizzes and tests. One of the best ways to *memorize* is to repeat out loud three times what needs to be remembered. For example, if your child were learning to spell "dog," he or she would say out loud three times, "d-o-g, d-o-g, d-o-g."

Try it yourself by picking out two lessons you have not yet read from either Chapter Six or Chapter Seven. Read the first lesson in the usual way to yourself. Then, tell someone else details about what you just read in that lesson.

Now read a second lesson, but this time, read the lesson *out loud* with good emphasis. Tell that person again all the details you can remember. I think you will agree that you recalled much more what you read aloud in the second lesson. Even though you did not read the lesson three times, you are involving three senses: seeing words through your eyes, hearing words through your ears, and speaking words with your mouth. Hopefully, this will make a significant difference for your child with tests and homework.

Shown below are seven additional ways to assist your child with a good academic effort.

- Arrive at the classroom early in order to get organized.
- Smile and say "Hi" to the teacher when you enter the classroom and when appropriate, tell the teacher "Thank you" and/or "Goodbye" when leaving the class.
- If possible, find a seat in the front row to diminish distractions.
- Keep eye contact with the teacher and attentively listen to the teacher's voice.
- Raise your hand and ask politely when you have questions and need help. Also, raise your hand when you can answer a teacher's question.

- Have good manners. When your teacher helps you, remember to say "Thank you" or "I appreciate . . ."
- If necessary, ask the teacher for help before or after school or check to see if extra credit work is available.

Another critical component for a good academic attitude is to teach your child, "Life is not fair and that also includes dealings with teachers, coaches, and the school."

Help your child understand that, to a certain degree, "Teachers don't have to get along with you, you need to get along with the teacher." Share with your child that acting disrespectfully will only hurt the relationship with the teacher. However, your child should let you know when the child thinks he or she is not being treated fairly, so you can assess the situation.

Until your child becomes responsible with completing homework, always check to ensure it was done. While counseling, a woman once told me, "My parents never asked about my grades or even if I had homework. My friends thought that my parents were cool. Now at forty-five, my life is all messed up."

With technology today, most schools post homework results online. If your child ever has difficulty completing homework, utilize the *You decided/Because/Try again* and *When you/Then you* parenting skills from Lessons 29 and 30.

At the end of the week, if your child has any incomplete assignments, I suggest you say, "***You decided*** not to have technology for this weekend ***because*** you have incomplete homework assignments. You can ***try again*** next week. The rule is '***When you*** complete all your homework during the week, ***then you*** may have technology on the weekend.'" I think you will be utterly amazed how motivated your child will become.

Positive thinking makes a momentous difference in terms of *academic success* for your child. I believe saying the following phrase out loud three times can recharge every person's attitude: "I can and I will today!" "I can and I will today!" "I can and I will today!" During breakfast or in the car on the way to school have your child say with you, "I can and I will today!" for a positive attitude to begin the day.

When my wife and I have the privilege of taking our three older grandchildren to school, before they enter the school building, we enthusiastically say that phrase with them three times. When my wife and I forget, they remind us which indicates just how much they benefit from those positive statements.

Now that you have this information, give a good consistent effort in leading and guiding your child toward ***consistent academic effort***! As an *Effective Parent*, always believe in your child's abilities and effort because that terrific encouragement will help him or her feel academically capable.

71. Homework Guidelines

An *Effective Parent* plays a major role in enhancing a child's positive school experience. A productive academic year is achieved through healthy homework guidelines. A homework environment that is similar to a school situation can support and supplement what takes place in the classroom for a child. Homework also teaches a child self-discipline and time management skills.

Homework is a reality in a student's life and should be viewed as an additional learning opportunity by both parents and child. A reasonable amount of homework supports the education experience, allowing a child to practice the skills and reinforce the knowledge learned in the classroom. At home, reinforce a learning attitude through when, where, and how to study guidelines. Sometimes for various reasons, a child may be hesitant to ask questions in the classroom, but he or she can easily ask his or her parents as homework is being completed.

Homework guidelines can assist a parent without nagging or constantly reminding a child about homework responsibility. In addition, the ***When you/Then you*** parenting skill is an excellent one to use with homework. Both parents and child are de-stressed by the calm, simple statement, "***When you*** finish your homework, ***then you*** may do something enjoyable."

It is not a question of will your child have homework, but how can homework guidelines enhance the growth and development of a child's study habits. Shown below are twelve guidelines that will enrich your child's homework experience.

1. ***Daily go through his or her backpack.*** Together with your elementary school child, review work, teacher's notes, assignments, and school announcements.
2. ***Allow for relaxation time***. Permit your child some time to unwind after school. After working all day, even adults desire some leisure time before beginning tasks at home.
3. ***Establish a homework routine.*** Basic guidelines provide a routine for healthy study habits that may make the education time more productive.
4. ***Daily study***. If all homework has been completed at school, each day have your child briefly review notes or reread material.
5. ***Regular time***. Try to have homework scheduled at the same time, Monday through Thursday. It makes no difference whether homework is done after school, before dinner, or after dinner, it is healthy to have a consistent routine. Involve your child in determining the best time to complete homework. At the beginning of the school year, perhaps experiment with different times every day the very first week.
6. ***No pressure***. Do not stress your child by treating homework as a goal to achieve or accomplish an excellent grade. School is stressful enough so the home needs to be a comfortable, safe environment where pressure is avoided, and learning can take place. Make your child's homework a comfortable activity.

7. ***Create independence***. Encourage your child to work independently without you monitoring and guiding the process. If necessary, study along with your child or sit next to him or her reading a book. However, striving for independence with homework is a healthy goal.
8. ***No distractions***. Like a classroom, it is usually a good idea for your child to study without having television, music, or technology gadgets on.
9. ***Location***. Have a location for your child to do homework with good lighting and necessary school supplies.
10. ***Review homework***. Look over the homework to check that it is neat and totally finished. Once your child has proven responsibility with completing homework, you may stop the review process.
11. ***Tests***. During homework time, help your child learn to study effectively for tests by reviewing notes out loud and utilizing past quizzes as study guides.
12. ***Limit technology on school nights***. On school nights, setting boundaries with television viewing, computer time, and tablet usage can diminish battles over homework. At the beginning of the school year decide those limits. Perhaps have a guideline of extra fun technology time for every minute of homework completed.

Please remember to express how proud you are of your child's efforts by displaying some of his or her schoolwork either on the refrigerator or a bulletin board. As with all areas of your child's life, focus more on his or her effort with homework, rather than performance or achievement. With appropriate guidelines, the homework process is an extremely valuable learning life experience.

72. Two Golden Questions with Report Cards

As an *Effective Parent*, one essential objective is for your child to fully understand and honestly believe that success academically has to do with his or her effort, improvement, and positive attitude toward school more than classroom performance and grades.

Two children could each give an "A-" effort academically and the outcome based on grades would be totally different simply because one child has a high IQ and the other a below-average IQ. Achievement and accomplishment are not profoundly important, but effort and ongoing improvement are absolutely significant for education and a successful life.

I have counseled nearly a thousand children and never once asked a child the grades he or she is earning. In fact, I often tell children, "Grades do not matter, all that counts is that you give an 'A-' effort in each of your classes." On the other hand, I have asked children and teenagers thousands of times about their effort grades for every one of their classes.

I think the best possible effort for any task or job is "A-" because every person is flawed and the world is imperfect. Due to living in a sinful world, an "A+" or "A" effort is impossible for every individual. Thinking "A+" or "A" also leads to perfectionistic thinking, which often creates anxiety, other emotional problems, and struggles in life.

I counseled a veterinarian with a successful practice who had tremendous anxiety because she was continually stressed attempting to be "A+" as a Christian, wife, mom, and in every other area of her life. When I helped her evaluate her parents' approach, she gained the insight that for both her and her parents, only "A+" was acceptable. This veterinarian said if she got even an "A-" on a test, her parents would ask, "What mistakes did you make that prevented you from earning an 'A+'?" From kindergarten to the present, she was extremely stressed thinking that she had to be a perfect "A+" in all aspects of life.

The goal for a child is to give an "A-" effort in every life endeavor and be proud when he or she achieves that goal. No person can absolutely determine an outcome, all that is possible is an "A-" effort. Understanding that concept has made a significant difference for so many I have counseled.

Based on the aforementioned knowledge, when you go through your child's report card, ask two questions about each class.

1. Will you please grade your effort in that subject from "A-" to "D-"?
2. If needed, what can you do to improve your effort in that subject? Assist your child in setting an improvement goal of one third of a letter grade.

With every student I counseled, I asked those exact two questions thousands of times. For example, "What was your effort grade in science?" If a student says "B-", I ask, "What will improve your effort to a 'B'?" Again, I only believe in seeking improvement in thirds rather than jumping all the way to an "A-" effort. A second example, "What was your effort grade in math?" If a teenager responds with "C+," I ask, "What can you do to improve your effort to a 'B-'?"

As an *Effective Parent*, with every report card, go through asking your child those same two questions with each subject. Hundreds of students have profusely thanked me for finally creating relaxed feelings with their educational endeavors.

In terms of encouragement, there is a difference in what a parent says to a *perfectionistic child* and an *unmotivated child*. If your child has perfectionistic tendencies, avoid telling that child, "Do your best." "Best" for a perfectionistic child is "A+," producing extreme stress and anxiety. With a *perfectionistic child*, encourage a "*good consistent 'A-' effort*" because that statement is destressing for a child who always strives for "A+." However, for an *unmotivated child,* you do want to encourage him or her with the statement "*Do your best.*" An unmotivated child needs that extra push of, "Do your best," in order to strive for an "A-" effort.

Utilizing the ***two golden questions*** allows for more encouragement with your child rather than criticism and correction. Your child will also feel more motivated at school because the pressure is removed for accomplishments and he or she can simply relax by *giving a good consistent "A-" effort.*

73. Productive Parent-Teacher Conferences

A *productive parent-teacher conference* is a valuable component for the educational welfare of your child. Most schools have several conferences that are fifteen minutes in length each academic year. The conference with your child's teacher will be more efficient and fruitful if you do some preparation beforehand.

Shown below are suggestions and questions to assist in preparing for the conference. Most of these recommendations are not necessarily new insights but are essential reminders.

Before the Conference

Prepare a list of questions for a constructive conversation with your child's teacher. Prioritize the questions under the following four major areas:

1. Behavioral
2. Academic
3. Social
4. Home Action Plan

Recognize you may only have three to four minutes for each of these key topics, so you will probably only be able to ask two to three questions in each area. Yet, always have enough questions in case you want to spend more time on one particular area.

Questions for Your Child Before the Conference

- What are some of the things you like and dislike about school?
- What are your easiest and hardest classes?
- What subjects do you like the least and the most?
- Are you having any problems in the classroom or with other students that you want me to discuss with the teacher? If your child mentions problems with classmates, do not take it as a sign of neglect by the teacher. Many times, your child either did not share that information with the teacher or the issues arose when the teacher was not around, like at recess.

At the Conference

Always arrive on time for the conference because teachers have busy schedules, and another conference is often scheduled right after your visit. Remember that the conference is a time to ask questions, listen, and learn how to assist your child. Be aware that the teacher will have his or her own agenda. Both you and the teacher want the best for your child!

Begin with a sincere appreciation for the teacher's hard work and care for your child. Like everyone, teachers appreciate genuine expressions of gratitude.

Ask your important questions early in the conference because it is often difficult to judge the fifteen-minute time limit. Stay calm and respectfully communicate throughout the conference. Getting upset will make it difficult to have a beneficial discussion.

Behavioral Questions About Your Child

- How are my child's attitude, self-confidence, and self-motivation?
- How are my child's manners and politeness?

- How well does my child respect you as a teacher?
- How does my child respect other teachers and classmates?
- What suggestions do you have regarding my child's behavior?

Academic Questions About Your Child

- What are my child's academic strengths and weaknesses?
- Is my child performing at, above, or below his or her grade level?
- How well is my child reaching academic potential?
- How well does my child use available study time during class?
- How often does my child participate in class?
- How well does my child handle academic setbacks?
- What are my child's strongest and weakest subjects?
- How often does my child hand homework in on time?
- How are my child's test-taking skills?
- If not explained in the student handbook, ask about the grading system.

Social Questions About Your Child

- How are my child's social skills?
- How easily does my child make friends? How many friends does my child have?
- How would you assess my child's friendships?
- Have you noticed any unusual behaviors around peers?
- What suggestions do you have for my child's social interactions with other children?
- How often does my child help other classmates?
- How well does my child handle social setbacks?

Questions to Establish a Home Action Plan

- What can I do at home to support my child's academic efforts?
- What specific suggestions can you offer me to help my child with behavioral issues, academic concerns, social skills, organization, etc.?
- What other recommendations do you have that will benefit my child?

Concluding the Parent-Teacher Conference

Just like at the start of the conference, enthusiastically thank the teacher for the time, encouragement of your child, and any specific things that the teacher did to help your child. Review the action plan with the teacher so you both have the same expectations for your child. Find out the best way to keep track of your child's school performance. Finally, ask the teacher the best way to communicate—email, text messages, phone, or written notes.

74. Helping an Academic Underachiever

An underachiever is NOT necessarily a child with low grades but a student who gives a substantially poor effort that results in grades lower than his or her abilities or intelligence quotient. No person ever feels good when he or she under-achieves any activity in life, so it is important to determine the reasons.

Most underachievers have a very weak self-image, have inadequate social skills, are often withdrawn, even shy around others, and lack confidence to experience even minor successes in any area of life. Or they may be just the opposite, angry, defiant, and rebellious especially during the teen years. Underachievers are usually overly critical of everyone including themselves. They may also brag and boast frequently about their "abilities" because they believe that builds their self-worth.

Academically, an underachiever usually lacks concentration, is easily distracted, is disorganized, has poor study habits, and the school effort is inconsistent. These children may also see school as too difficult and believe they are not smart enough.

Due to not having minor successes in school, feelings of hopelessness and helplessness dominate their mind. This causes underachievers to appear lazy because they easily give up, thus, spending countless hours watching television, playing video games, listening to music, or something other than studying. A vicious negative cycle begins because when they do not try, the result is almost no accomplishments and that lowers their self-worth even more.

A major problem for this child and the parents is setting unrealistic goals or having no plan at all on how to take steps towards improvement. Always ensure success for an underachieving child by setting small, incremental goals which allow him or her to succeed. A small goal may be bringing the appropriate books home and/or homework. Another goal is completing daily homework even if test scores and quizzes continue to be low. Involve an underachiever in activities outside school where minor successes may help the child begin to thrive in his or her eyes.

The lessons in Chapter Two are important for every child, but they are critically vital for an underachieving child. More than ever, an underachieving child needs unconditional verbal and physical love. Daily, this child needs numerous *Appreciation Vitamins* when exhibiting persistence and determination with any school task. Focusing on wonderful effort and praising improvement is a major parenting goal for building an underachiever's self-confidence.

Try to determine the specific reasons for underachievement, such as, incomplete homework, behavior issues in class, poor influence of classmates, physical disabilities, learning problems, etc. Maybe an underachiever needs to be tested for learning disorders. If necessary, schedule a conference with your child's teacher, the school counselor, and the principal.

Most underachievers read at a very low grade level. Becoming a great reader should be one of the first goals for an underachiever. If reading is an issue, ask the school for assistance in elevating reading skills through computer programs or outside assistance.

Absolutely avoid being upset or, even worse, angry because that will diminish even further a child's self-confidence and hurt the parent-child relationship. Do not nag or criticize, but use the "When you/Then you" parenting skill to encourage completion of school responsibilities. In addition, avoid being overprotective by offering homework answers because that only fosters poor performance.

For whatever reason, some underachievers are motivated by technology privileges. After giving a good effort, showing improvement, and completing homework, at times allow for another thirty minutes of technology time even on a school night.

There are times when a change of schools, or even a change of teachers within a school, can significantly benefit an underachiever. When I was vice president at Concordia Theological Seminary, I would regularly meet with incoming seminarians and their wives to enhance the transition process to a new city.

When a couple had children, I would ask if they had any academic concerns. Parents would sometimes respond with, "We think the transition will be smooth for Paul because he has many friends and is a good student. However, we are concerned for Pam because she lacks friendships and underachieves in school." Surprisingly, the reverse often happened, where Paul struggled, and Pam flourished in the new school. The dynamics of social relationships, teachers, classroom environment, etc. negatively impacted one child, while the other made a total positive turnaround. A fresh start in a different classroom or even a new school may make a positive difference for some underachievers.

A major goal for a parent is to lower expectations when implementing various new approaches and ideas. Helping an underachiever may require one to two years. Set a small goal of one percent improvement per week for a child. Of course, that is only four percent each month, but remarkably, fifty percent progress by the end of one year.

The significant goal for an underachiever is to feel good about his or her effort and continually strive for improvement. Keep in mind, some underachievers do not attend college but pursue technical schools where they gain skills for excellent careers in nonacademic professions.

Finally, *BE PATIENT* with yourself and your child!

75. School Attendance: Three Guidelines

In counseling, hundreds of parents have shared, "At times, my child tells me he or she is sick and doesn't want to attend school on some days. I want to believe my child but how can I make a healthy decision for my child when I am not sure if he or she is truly physically sick?"

When a person is sick, that person feels uncomfortable to varying degrees. Employed adults are only allowed so many sick and vacation days. An ill adult decides to be uncomfortable either at home or work, often based upon how many sick and/or vacation days are available. Keep in mind most children will not have the pain tolerance of an adult.

Sooner than later, a child needs to learn to cope with the pain of minor illnesses, be uncomfortable, and still be involved with daily activities, including school. Aches, pains, and the common cold are part of life and persistence in attending school is part of the developmental process toward adulthood. Whether at home or school, a child will not always feel 100 percent well. A child learns determination when he or she goes to school even though he or she may not be feeling 100 percent physically healthy.

An *Effective Parent* does not coddle but desires to instill strong character, inner strength, and determination for the sake of the child's present and future life. Hence, when a child is not feeling 100 percent, these guidelines may assist a parent with commonsense wisdom in helping a child fulfill significant life obligations like attending school.

However, at times, problems like generalized anxiety disorder, depression, social anxiety, or other mental struggles often creates an unwillingness or inability within that child to attend school because he or she does not have the emotional strength.

Shown below are three recommendations that have benefited numerous parents in handling a child's reported illness. However, check with your child's school to determine the health guidelines.

1. ***Fever.*** A child should not go to school with a fever. If a child has a fever, most schools want a child to be fever-free for at least twenty-four hours before returning. However, if a child has a cold with no fever, then school is probably the appropriate option.
2. ***Vomiting or diarrhea.*** A child should be free of vomiting or diarrhea for at least twenty-four hours before returning to school.
3. ***Significant illnesses***. A child with serious and contagious illnesses like measles, chicken pox, pinkeye, etc. should not attend school.

With perceived illnesses, it is challenging to make the best decision for your child, other children, and teachers at school. These three suggestions are simple guidelines to ensure the best possible outcome for everyone when a child reports an illness to the parent. Truly, your child can benefit from participating in important activities like school even if he or she is not feeling 100 percent, a responsible decision for life.

76. Curfew

Curfews create a safe environment, teaching a child time management and decision-making skills. Curfews help a child get enough sleep so he or she can accomplish personal responsibilities the next day.

When your children leave home for whatever reason, it is a good idea to know:

- Where are they going?
- What are they doing?
- Who will be with them?
- When will they be home?

A curfew during the week is based on homework, necessary sleep, and justifiable reasons for going out. At times, a curfew may be based upon your child's demonstration of responsibility and maturity rather than age. Shown below are suggested *maximum* weekend curfew times determined by high school grade.

9th grade: 11:00 p.m. to 11:30 p.m.
10th grade: 11:30 p.m. to 12 midnight
11th grade: 12:00 midnight to 12:30 a.m.
12th grade: 12:30 a.m. to 1:00 a.m.

Just because these are maximum curfews does not mean your child has to stay out that late if he or she doesn't have specific plans with scheduled activities for the evening. For example, a ninth grader may say, "I am going out with friends but not sure what we are doing for the evening." Unscheduled time often leads to mischief and a parent, in this case, may not allow the maximum curfew of 11:00 p.m. to 11:30 p.m.

However, if the ninth grader said, "I am going to the football game with my friends, then we will meet at a pizza place, and I will be home between 11:00 p.m. and 11:30 p.m." This would be acceptable because there is a plan for the entire evening.

Many parents may fear a curfew of 12:30 a.m. for a twelfth grader, but after high school, a child is on his or her own and will decide how late he or she stays out, perhaps even 3:00 or 4:00 a.m. Parents who understand that principle help the child by increasing responsibility with each high school year.

Please remember that, after high school, most individuals go to college, get a job, or move into an apartment. On their own, they determine their curfew and how to valuably use time. Setting and gradually expanding the curfew time during the high school years can assist your child in making responsible decisions with time as an adult.

77. Watch Your Child's Friendships

Every *Effective Parent* wants a child to stay on a Biblical path of values. For your child to remain within the boundaries God provides in the Bible, selecting friends with a positive moral outlook on life will be a necessity. Proverbs 13:20 encourages, "Walk with the wise and become wise, for a companion of fools suffers harm" (NIV).

Friendships will play a major role in influencing your child's moral character and choices in life. When I was a Lutheran high school teacher, we did an informal survey of our ninth graders asking who had the greatest influence on their decision-making. Friends were first by a large margin and parents were a distant second. Fully understand your child will become very similar to the five friends he or she associates with the most.

A wise parent will ***watch closely his or her child's friendships,*** while at the same time, giving freedom in that selection process. Lovingly guide your child in finding Godly friends. Teach your child that peer pressure is a two-way street, where he or she can take the lead in making responsible decisions to influence others.

I have counseled wonderful children raised by excellent parents who became part of a bad crowd with devastating results. A problem friendship may create negative tendencies in your child with a quick spiral downward. Be subtle by asking your child a lot of "How" and "What" questions to assist your child in gaining a true perspective of a problematic friend. Do not try to cut off toxic friendships, but instead, try to gradually phase them out by encouraging your child to connect with healthier kids. Perhaps, intervene by having your child invite healthy kids that make good decisions to your house.

Every *Effective Parent* must initiate knowing a child's friends. Have your child invite friends to your house, so you can observe their actions and words. When your child has a friend over, you can also observe how your child does implementing social skills.

After meeting your child's friend(s) ask yourself several questions:

- Do they have good manners?
- Are they respectful?
- How does the friend treat your child and speak about others?
- Do they make positive comments about school?
- Without interrogating, does their family regularly attend church?
- How is their grooming?
- After spending time with a particular friend, is your child usually still happy and kind toward you?

Although not an exhaustive list, these are important questions that assist a parent in assessing if your child is choosing friends with high character qualities.

Personally, get to know the parents of your child's friends. Children are often remarkably similar to one or both parents. Communication is the key, so at a minimum, speak to parents of your child's friends on the phone. When appropriate, have your child's friends' parents over for dinner to learn their values, life perspective, the rules in their home, and attitude about church attendance. If their values are markedly different, lovingly steer your child toward other friendships.

In addition, never allow your child to enter the house of a friend until you know the parents very well. In counseling, children and teens have reported going into a friend's house to watch pornography and drink alcohol, while their parents thought they were in a "safe" environment.

When your child goes to a friend's house, if possible, it is a good idea for your child to have a cell phone with him or her. If an emergency arises, your child can easily call you just as you can also talk to him or her when necessary. Always have the phone number of the parents whose home your child is visiting.

Making friends is a vital part of life. Always attempt to ensure that your child's friends build your child up, not tear him or her down! When your child surrounds himself or herself with the right kind of friends, automatically, that has a positive impact on values, character, and decision-making. As an *Effective Parent*, teach your child both how to make friends, as well as what critical qualities to look for in a healthy friend.

78. Ask "WHY," Don't "Just Say No"

Jesus mostly taught with questions instead of statements. Jesus asked questions for a variety of reasons, but they always had a purpose. Jesus asked questions of others to:

Inform -- Mark 8:5
Discern -- Matthew 16:14
Teach -- Matthew 6:27
Encourage -- John 11:40

After calming the storm, Jesus even asked questions to challenge the apostles in Matthew 8:26 with, "*Why* are you afraid? You have so little faith" (NLT). In the Sermon on the Mount, Jesus asked, "*Why* are you anxious about clothes?" (Matthew 6:28 NIV) and "*Why* do you see the piece of sawdust in another believer's eye and not notice the wooden beam in your own eye?" (Matthew 7:3 GW). The word "Why" is a personal challenge for the other individual to identify what they are thinking or doing wrong.

The "*Just Say No*" slogan was extremely popular in the eighties and nineties as a tactic to encourage kids to reject offers to use alcohol and drugs. I applaud the campaign, but it was basically ineffective because the reply to "No" is often "Why not?"—a much more powerful response! Although I admire the crusade, saying "No" actually sets up a child to be on the defensive because the other person is going to come back with, "Why not?"

Frequently discuss moral issues with your child to assist him or her in gaining your Biblical perspective. Abstaining from nicotine, alcohol, drugs, sex, etc. will be a difficult challenge for your child as it is for everyone. In that regard, one of the best skills you can teach your child to resist peer pressure and avoid falling prey to numerous temptations is to utilize the question, "Why?" Asking "Why" implies that the other person's motives are questionable for even suggesting the temptation.

For example, an unhealthy youngster offers your child a cigarette and he or she appropriately answers with "No." Immediately, the tempter could ask "Why not?" Your child may respond with, "My parents say cigarettes are not good for me," and the other child could ask, "*Why* does that matter?" If your child says, "It is against the law," the questioner could ask, "*Why* do we care about the law?" If your child responds that, "Cigarettes are not healthy," the harmful child could ask, "*Why* will one cigarette hurt you?" So, you understand that when your child says "No" almost immediately he or she is on the defensive and forced to come up with excellent reasons for saying "No" over and over.

"Why" is the magical word that makes it so much easier for your child to stand up to peer pressure. Let me reverse roles in the aforementioned example to show how asking "Why" can be a difference maker when resisting temptations.

The harmful friend says, "Let's smoke a cigarette together." If your child responds with "Why" the unwholesome friend may say, "Because we will be cool." Again, if your child firmly asks, "Why?" the damaging friend is taken off guard and might say, "We will feel good by breaking the law." Then, your child could confidently ask, "Why?" The unhealthy friend in frustration might state, "The other kids at school will think we are grown-up." And again, your child could assertively ask, "Why?" Finally, exasperated, the unhealthy youngster may just give up. Your child will experience a healthy pride of how he or she resisted temptation and feel confident about defying future invitations to do the wrong thing.

As an *Effective Parent*, role play with your child where you are the unhealthy friend offering the temptation. At different times, role play over and over with not only cigarettes but alcohol, marijuana, vaping, pornography, sexual advances, etc. Your child can never have too much practice asking, "Why?"

Parents have told me they role played with their sons and daughters how to resist sexual advances. In counseling, teenagers who have learned to use this important skill have said it is so funny when they rejected the sexual advance and asked "Why?" They reported the other teen is used to hearing "No," and that asking "Why" catches the teen off guard. He or she can't think of a good answer, and eventually just stops making advances.

Every child faces temptation so the individual question is, "How can I stand strong and overcome them?" Certainly, if there was an easy answer to that question, resisting the lure of sin would not be a problem. Nonetheless, the invaluable skill of asking "**Why**" can make a significant difference for your child when it comes to peer pressure and temptations.

79. Modest Personal Appearance

Modesty is a virtue that takes courage and seems to be significantly absent in society today. A child's focus over personal appearance usually continues to grow as he or she becomes older. What is always most important for your child is to develop internal qualities. A modest child displays a wholesome appearance that overcomes the desire to look "sexy" on the outside.

The Bible confirms that goal, "Don't be concerned about the outward beauty of fancy hairstyles, expensive jewelry, or beautiful clothes. You should clothe yourselves instead with the beauty that comes from within, the unfading beauty of a gentle and quiet spirit, which is so precious to God" (1 Peter 3:4 NLT).

Our loving God is only concerned with inward virtues because beauty is only skin-deep while character goes right to the bone. Guide your child to understand that improving internal attributes is the goal which is achieved by not being overly concerned with outward attractiveness.

Due to technology, social media, and advertisements, many unrealistic expectations are placed on a child's appearance. Today, children are assaulted by the fashion world, television, movies, and the internet suggesting that the focus is only on outward appearances. Some fashion retailers, television shows, and Hollywood companies have also inappropriately started sexualizing children with dress that is far from modest. Children are posing in provocative adult clothing that damages their youthful innocence, often leading to promiscuous teen years and a struggling adult life.

Such an unhealthy preoccupation with seductive clothing and make-up negatively impacts a child's inner beauty, often leading to sexual immorality. An immodest appearance may often send clues of seductiveness that perhaps were unintentional, but induce ideas of sinful fantasy in others. A seductive appearance also puts a child at risk with a sexual predator.

An *Effective Parent* wisely recognizes a provocative physical appearance hurts the child now and potentially as an adult. Remind your child often of the importance for modesty to influence Godly character within. A child's modest physical appearance helps to effectively oppose the temptations he or she faces while strengthening his or her ability to make healthy choices. Being modest often builds a wall that discourages sexual acting out.

Whenever a child is overly concerned with the perfect body image, especially being thin or small, that thinking may easily create an eating disorder. A child with an eating disorder has a distorted perception of his or her physical appearance that only increases negative thoughts and personal dissatisfaction, while diminishing the importance of internal values.

When the toxic media world exposes your child to glamourous sexual styles, gently explain the negative influence of that message on being a modest person. Set modesty standards early by teaching your child to have self-respect by keeping his or her body "private" from others. Parading one's body in front of others, even family members, is not healthy, while maintaining privacy creates beneficial internal modesty. Modesty can be instilled in a child by having him or her change clothes in private and closing the door when using the bathroom. Parents need to follow those same guidelines as well.

Sadly, I have counseled adults who grew up with nudity and immodest attire frequently exhibited in the home resulting in having boundary difficulties, identity issues, and sexual intimacy struggles.

A child must learn that seeking an alluring appearance rarely infuses self-respect and modesty.

Modesty flows from a humble, pure spirit that values attractiveness but does not seek to be provocative. Shop with your child to show him or her that clothing can be stylish yet modest. Frequently tell your child how beautiful he or she is on the inside to boost self-esteem.

As an *Effective Parent*, don't be overly preoccupied with your physical appearance but strive to dress tastefully so that your child witnesses modesty in action. Model your values through your own fashion choices that uphold Godly standards. Help your child keep a solid modesty perspective by reminding him or her that one's identity and significance is determined not by clothing or body image but by inner beauty.

80. Television and Video Games

After counseling and speaking to thousands of parents, I found that a major challenge for many moms and dads is the amount of television and video game time for their child. Both parents often base their thinking on the amount of time they personally spent on both during childhood, creating stress over what is acceptable.

Do not be guided by *fluctuating studies* on screen time that change year to year. During the COVID pandemic, many children did schoolwork on a computer or tablet at home for over six hours a day.

Television and video games are fine for a child if they are entertainment and hobbies, not obsessions or compulsive behaviors. Television and video games are only two activities in the midst of numerous possibilities like playing outdoors, homework, family games, sports in the neighborhood, reading time, etc. When any hobby or pastime produces excessive inactivity, insufficient social interaction, or a broad lack of interests, then those activities are probably obsessions or addictions.

Many parents take an almost all-or-nothing approach with television and video games, meaning, either they allow *extraordinarily little* or have *no limits* on the amount of time. Like with most interests, having an extreme policy on TV or video game time is detrimental for a child. As with nearly all life activities, moderation is the key versus an inflexible, extreme position. Keep in mind, violent or sexually provocative video games are not healthy for a child.

Play is part of childhood and that includes video games. Like adults, children need to unwind from academics and chore responsibilities. Besides being a fun, leisure activity, wholesome video games have benefits. Video games are often designed on the principle of problem-solving that enhances a child's critical thinking in learning to find solutions. One of the greatest qualities a child needs to strengthen is determination, which may be gained through healthy gaming. Reaction time and hand-eye coordination are necessary skills when playing sports. Both are developed through video games.

Watching television has benefits and is enjoyable when there are reasonable guidelines. Use parental controls to block inappropriate channels, as well as choosing the right kind of content. Sex, crime, and violence are prevalent on television. Viewing sex may lead to promiscuity, while violence may make some kids more aggressive. In addition, keep television, video games, computer, and other electronics out of the bedroom, so a child does not isolate or view unacceptable material.

A parent viewing worthwhile television with the child allows for emotional bonding, possible physical touch, and conversation. Laughing together is so especially important for every family, which easily happens while watching comedy programs and movies. There are also educational programs regarding science, wildlife, sports, and geography.

In terms of time with television and video games, develop two sets of rules, one for the week and the other for the weekend. During the school week, a general rule is a daily maximum of two hours, while on the weekend, a total of four hours per day. Yet, be flexible when there are special programs or events. For example, a child and parent watching a college or professional sports event, lengthy movie, documentary, NASCAR race, etc. may spend two to four hours bonding together over that program. When using time as a guideline, with each passing year as your child ages, re-evaluate the rules to allow the child to eventually make his or her own TV and video game decisions as a high schooler.

Another valuable method to determine the amount of time for television and video games is to utilize five questions to assess if your child has a balanced life.

1. How many hobbies, sports activities, outside play time, general exercise, etc. is my child involved in?
2. How often does my child interact socially with other children?
3. How is my child's school effort in completing homework as well as staying focused at school?
4. How healthy is my child physically, meaning, is he or she fit or overweight?
5. Does my child regularly get a good night's sleep?

When the answers to those questions are satisfactory, then a child is probably not watching too much television or playing too many video games.

Hopefully, these suggestions can bring both parents together in establishing appropriate yet flexible guidelines. Setting reasonable limits will diminish family stress and guide your child toward making healthy decisions with television and video games as an adult.

81. Internet and Social Media

The Internet and social media have no physical borders, opening a child to an entire world of potential negative influence. However, there are benefits like information, knowledge, entertainment, and connecting with others. Nonetheless, the negatives are almost endless, including cyberbullying, cyber predators, stalkers, pornography, online scams, social isolation, damage to a child's emotional well-being, addiction, suicidal ideation, gambling, etc. Although the negatives may outweigh the positives, children will still want to use the internet and social media.

Many studies point out that the internet could damage children through sexual solicitation, emails from strangers, and mental manipulation within harmful chat rooms. The percentages vary, but before the age of eighteen, approximately 90 percent of children will view pornography on the internet and more than 50 percent will receive emails from a stranger. When a child has few friends, is isolated, and feels hopeless, he or she is especially vulnerable to the possible "toxins" promoted through the internet and social media.

Your child should be taught to never look at another person's cell phone unless he or she is with you. Sadly, I counseled a six-year-old boy who had not learned that guideline and saw explicit porn on another boy's cell phone. The first week of school, an older child on the school bus had a cell phone with a porn movie and passed the phone around to all the other children on the bus. Truly sad for this wonderful Christian young man, his parents, and all the other children! Each child on that school bus was sexually traumatized, potentially harming his or her future perspective of sexual intimacy.

This six-year-old's parents had done an exceptionally fine job of educating him regarding the potential problems with the internet and social media. However, they did not discuss boundaries with another child's cell phone.

I counseled a fourteen-year-old girl whose loving parents trusted too much and did not monitor any of her online activities. Through a "poisonous" chatroom, she became very attached and thought she was in "love" with a "seventeen-year-old boy" in California. She actually purchased an airline ticket to fly to

California to visit him, but just before she boarded the airplane, the police were able to "save" her. The "seventeen-year-old young man" was actually a prostitution ring that played on the emotions of young girls, convincing them to fly to California. Once in California, they were given cocaine and heroin to be controlled with drugs, turning them into prostitutes.

Your child also must be taught the dangers associated with sharing cell phone pictures and videos because they can easily be shared with the world. Teach your child to fully understand that there is no delete key when personal information is posted in any form.

I counseled a teenage girl who had suicidal thoughts because her ex-boyfriend and this young lady had taken a video of a sexual act together on his cell phone. When she broke up with him, the ex-boyfriend, in retaliation, shared the sexual video with numerous teenagers at their high school. The shame and guilt produced suicidal ideation in this teenage girl and made it difficult for her to even attend school because it was such a horrific, traumatizing experience. Thankfully, her depression lifted when she implemented positive words and behaviors that I suggested for her.

As an *Effective Parent*, continually educate yourself on the rapid changes occurring with the internet and social media. Your child may be extremely responsible but still monitor his or her online and social media activity. Although not exhaustive, shown below are "Guidance for a Parent" and "Rules for a Child" to provide boundaries.

Guidance for a Parent

- Educate your child early and often about the dangers of the internet and social media.
- Install online protection tools to provide security.

- Establish limits and set rules so your child knows what you expect.
- Have your child use computers, tablets, etc. in the common area of the home.
- Frequently check your child's browser history.
- Share your child's email account.
- Have your child friend you on Facebook, Instagram, Twitter, etc.
- No downloading new apps without your approval.
- Have your child tell you *everything* that happens on the internet, like strangers contacting him or her, someone wanting to send a gift, etc.
- Whenever your child goes to a friend's house, always ask if he or she is allowed internet access.
- Be on high alert when you walk by your child and he or she suddenly shuts down the computer.
- When a child does not talk about his or her online activities or suddenly withdraws from family life be aware something is not right.
- Computers, tablets, and cell phones should be included in the amount of screen time allowed.

Rules for a Child

- Have your child communicate with you immediately when he or she receives threats, scary comments, or uncomfortable information.
- Know your child's passwords and tell him or her not to share passwords with anyone.
- Never reveal personal information and perhaps only use a screen name.
- Never post personal pictures without your permission.
- Do not talk to strangers on the internet.

- No entering a chat room without your permission, and then, it is probably best to enter that chat room together. Only chat with people you know.
- Always ask permission before downloading or uploading anything.
- No clicking on ads or offsite links without permission.
- Never meet with anyone personally who contacted him or her online.

Today, nearly every child becomes a technology expert at an early age, making it difficult for a parent to supervise everything. You can keep up with your child's social media life, monitor computer time, educate often, and have the absolute best rules, but your child can still fall prey to temptations and overcome your limits. Nonetheless, be aware of your child's daily online activities and strive to continuously learn the latest ways on how to protect your child from the dangers of online access.

82. Chemical Temptations

This lesson will provide a brief overview in helping your child cope with chemical temptations. Throughout the lesson, when the word "chemicals" is used, it will be all encompassing to include nicotine, alcohol, and drugs.

Kids today face a much harsher world and are seriously threatened not just by the internet and social media but also chemical temptations. Preparing your child to cope with the real world of chemicals is a difficult challenge. Proverbs 4:23 declares, "Guard our heart above all else, for it determines the course of your life" (NLT). What flows out of the heart or "thoughts" are actions. Your goal is to "guard" and influence your child's heart to guide your child toward good choices, particularly when it comes to chemicals.

Being an excellent parental role model is always essential but setting a healthy example when it comes to chemicals is even more impactful on a child. To help your child avoid life-damaging chemicals, always be a model of the behavior you want to see in your child. If you do drink alcohol, do so infrequently, in moderation, and do not have an abundance of alcohol in your home. From an early age, educate your child to stay away from nicotine products and drugs.

Trust and mutual respect ensure good two-way conversation, especially when it comes to discussing chemicals with your child!

When communicating with your child, it is essential to be compassionate, understanding, and have a loving tone. When discussing chemicals, it is best to ask numerous “How” and “What” questions, so that your child comes up with the answers on his or her own. Ask questions like: “What is your opinion about smoking cigarettes, drinking alcohol, and using drugs?” “What are good reasons not to get involved with cigarettes, alcohol, and drugs?” “How can chemicals negatively impact your life?”

In addition, role play with the “Why” question (Lesson 78) regarding nicotine, alcohol, and drugs. At the end of discussions, share appropriate information about the dangers of all three chemicals but do not lecture! Teach your child that whatever decisions he or she makes today with chemicals may adversely affect his or her future in terms of relationships and, perhaps, even increased health risks like cancer, heart attack, and stroke in adulthood.

Absolutely do not tell your child about your experiences as a teen with cigarettes, alcohol, drugs, or even sex. Incorrectly, too many parents think that sharing their past will cause a child to avoid making big mistakes.

If you told your child you *never tried* nicotine, alcohol, or drugs, and your child had already experimented with one of those chemicals, he or she may have lower self-worth because he or she fell short and was not as good as you. Even worse, if you told your child you *did experiment* with chemicals, that almost always gives a teen a ready-made excuse to think his or her mom or dad used "chemicals," so there is nothing wrong with me continuing to use nicotine, alcohol, or drugs as well.

I have never counseled one teenager that stopped using chemicals because the parents told the teen they experimented with them. Again, just the opposite usually happened where the teenager thought, "My mom or dad did it, so no big deal," giving the teenager a justification to increase the frequency of using chemicals.

Be completely prepared if your child does ask if you smoked cigarettes, drank alcohol, or tried drugs as a teenager. Have an answer planned well in advance. I suggest saying something like, "Do not compare yourself to me, your friends, or anyone else because what's important is making responsible decisions in all areas of your life, and chemicals are not good choices. Comparisons are totally not healthy and the only comparison you and I or any person should ever make is with Jesus. Certainly, you and I do not measure up to Jesus nor does anyone but thankfully we are forever forgiven! I believe in you and have confidence that you will make good choices when it comes to avoiding chemicals."

What is most important is to absolutely acknowledge every child can give into the temptation of chemicals because "No one is good—except God alone" (Mark 10:18 NIV). There are many reasons for a child to use chemicals. Most teens believe nothing can harm them, so there is often no fear for the present, much less a concern for how current bad choices may negatively impact their future adult life. Your teen may be smart and a good student but that does not necessarily mean he or she will automatically demonstrate mature choices with chemicals. Many times, a child struggling with anxiety or depression will try chemicals to self-medicate, hoping to escape problems.

Be aware that peers are the greatest influence in a child's decision-making, including avoiding chemicals. Recognize that social transitions like going from elementary school to middle school or middle school to high school are vulnerable times because new friendships, sometimes unhealthy ones, are developed. Friends who are in trouble with the law, doing poorly in school, etc. often use chemicals, which may pull your child down with them.

Legal drugs like painkillers and other prescription medications are a serious problem, especially with athletes who have been injured but think numbing the pain will help them recover faster.

It is key to evaluate if the use is experimental, social, regular, or an addictive dependency. Be aware of changes in a teen because that is often the first signal that a chemical problem exists. Some signs of chemical abuse are:

- Poor academic performance
- Irritability
- Decreased interest in activities
- Diminished personal appearance
- Red eyes
- Secretive behavior
- Negative attitude
- Tiredness
- Withdrawal from family members
- Unexplained need for money

When a teenager is involved with chemicals, appropriate consequences or taking away privileges are often beneficial. However, there is a fine line between corrective discipline that is too lengthy or too brief. The goal is to have a positive impact on the teen, so better choices are made in the future.

Many years ago, I was on a drug task force at a Christian high school. Two police officers shared with our group that teens from financially comfortable homes are more likely to use alcohol and drugs because they have the money to do so. They suggested parents keep track of their cash, because when children take money from a parent's wallet, some parents often do not realize that twenty or fifty dollars is missing.

Many parents have asked in counseling if it is okay to go through their child's room and "stuff"? The answer is "Yes" when a parent has concerns.

The police will not search a home unless they have probable cause that the owners are doing something wrong. Likewise, when a parent sees "signs of chemical abuse," it is very important to search the child's room, car, and "stuff" so the parent can immediately address the problem. When a parent believes a teen is using a chemical, always go through his or her backpack because that is often where teens keep cigarettes, drugs, and drug paraphernalia.

Please understand when chemical use is prevalent, it is normal for a teen to frequently lie. Chemical users are also often unstructured and disorganized, so an important objective is to develop daily routines and structure to make a positive change.

When a teen is using chemicals, a parent's most important goal is to remain calm, be respectful, and demonstrate love rather than anger. A parent is *not* dealing with a ***problem teen*** but a ***teen with a problem*** who needs help. Focus on the poor choices, not the teen as a person.

I pray that chemicals never become a significant issue for your child. If they do, use the ideas that are suggested in this lesson. When a teenager is involved with chemicals, it is usually beneficial to seek outside counsel, particularly with a chemical expert.

83. Dating Guidelines

Dating depends on the maturity level of your teenager as well as age because both are important in terms of when to begin. When your child's heart (Proverbs 4:23) is right usually his or her decision-making is healthy most of the time. Dating requires a lot of major choices with the opposite sex including some that can impact a teen's entire life.

Determining the correct time for a teenager to date is a difficult decision for every parent. In trying to assess if any type of dating is an option, the first question to consider would be, "Is my teenager capable of making responsible choices with a member of the opposite sex?" Many ninth graders in high school want to begin dating. Under the age of sixteen, encourage going out in groups versus one-on-one dating. Sadly, too many parents also do not inform their teen that any sexual contact outside of marriage goes against Biblical values.

There is a direct correlation between the teenager's age at the first date and when he or she starts sexual activity. A teen that begins one-on-one dating between the ages of thirteen to fifteen has a high probability of early sexual experiences before he or she finishes high school. When a teenager starts dating at the age of sixteen or later, the possibility for sexual activity before high school graduation seems to decrease significantly.

Whatever the age, verbalize your faith and trust in your teen's decision making. Make a comment like, "I want you to know that my trust is in you. My confidence is in God to guide you. I respect you and believe that you will make good choices." Every time your teenager goes on a date, there should be a plan for the entire evening so as not to allow for any free, mischief time. At sixteen and seventeen, rarely is it a good idea to have a four-to-five-hour date because having an entire evening together may easily lead to feeling pressure for unwholesome physical activities.

Discuss with your teenager that holding hands is fine and, after several dates perhaps, quick kisses may be acceptable. However, teach your teen to avoid lengthy kisses and open mouth kisses because that often leads to difficult choices including intercourse. Lovingly emphasize to your teenager that, when someone cares for you and respects you, he or she will only do what is in your best interests.

It would be great for a teen to begin dating after completing high school, but that is frequently unrealistic.

When your teenager begins showing an interest in the opposite sex, have him or her fulfill what I call an "Assessment Activity." Ask your teen to write down *fifteen qualities* he or she thinks are important in a person of the opposite sex, and more specifically, a future spouse. Some virtues that might be listed include: self-control, forgiving spirit, good student, good communicator, responsible, kind, patient, respectful, is encouraging of others, etc.

Hopefully, the positive attributes will be internal, not external, but that often is not the case. The younger the teenager, the more likely the list will include handsome, good figure, beautiful eyes, nice legs, big breasts, muscles, etc. Attraction is important but that does not lead to a lasting relationship. In counseling, when I review a person's "Assessment Activity," I stress the main focus should be on internal qualities because that has a greater likelihood of being present for a lifetime.

I jokingly tell people that, although I played college sports with muscles and hair on my head (I am mostly bald now), if my wife liked me for those external attributes, she would be disappointed because those two physical traits are absent today.

The remainder of the "Assessment Activity" is for a teen to write down a minimum of *five intolerable flaws* or *deal breakers* that would cause him or her not to date a particular person of the opposite sex. The *five intolerable flaws* may be more important than the *fifteen qualities*. Adults will often include on the list: temper, self-centered, addictions, financially irresponsible, alcoholic, unforgiving, lazy, verbally abusive, etc. A teenager may write down those adult possibilities and may include as well, troublemaker, obnoxious, disrespectful, poor academic effort, crude, gossiper, liar, etc.

Initially, some parents think this is a judgmental activity. However, being judgmental is feeling superior or looking down on someone. Assessing or evaluating is determining if a relationship will build up or tear down your teen's character.

Once your teenager wants to date, you can easily ask, "How does that person compare to your *fifteen qualities* and *five intolerable flaws* list?" The "Assessment Activity" is just one more way to lead and guide your teen toward a healthy relationship, thus, diminishing potential problems.

You can establish guidelines, but realize that your teenager may still try to do some form of dating without your knowledge. Thus, always be willing to discuss and LISTEN to your teen's feelings. Threats and overreactions will only drive a wedge in your relationship and sometimes push a teenager to make unhealthy dating decisions.

84. God's Gift of Sex

The importance of caring for the body God gave us is highlighted in 1 Corinthians 6:19, "Don't you realize that your body is the temple of the Holy Spirit, who lives in you and was given to you by God"(NLT)? This lesson focuses on *protecting* a child's body or "temple" and *saving* one's body sexually for the confines of marriage.

Educating your child to ***protect him or her from sexual abuse*** is essential!

Studies vary, but nearly one-third of girls and one-fifth of boys will be sexually abused before the age of eighteen. Most sexual abuse occurs in a child's home, by a person who has a trusting relationship with the child, or by an immature individual with low self-esteem. Some danger signals of having been sexually abused are:

- Low self-esteem
- Emotionally upset at the slightest problem
- Overly pleasing behavior
- Anxious
- Depressed
- Sleep difficulties

- Easily frightened

Your child needs to be taught that no one may touch his or her private areas or parts of the body under a bathing suit. Three key talking points are:

1. *Confusing touches* that initially feel good but then begin to feel bad inside
2. *Good touches* like nice hugs versus *bad touches* that make you feel internally sick
3. *Okay touches* versus *not okay touches*

Teach your child that if anyone, including a family member, tries to touch a private body part, *your child should look that person directly in the eyes,* ***firmly shout "NO,"*** *and then run away.* Always emphasize that your child is not to blame, but the other person or perpetrator is totally wrong and doing something very terrible or bad.

Private time between children should always be closely supervised. I have had hundreds of adult counselees share that they were either sexually abused or experimented sexually with another child while the parents were in the other room. Many of these tragic situations occurred with siblings, cousins, or family friends.

Always be extra vigilant when allowing children to be alone together because that is when sexual problems often arise. Have the vital goal of watching closely time alone between your child and other children even of the same sex. Sleepovers have also led to sexual problems for many I have counseled.

Teaching about *God's gift of sex* is best accomplished through Christian books that can be read to a child at various ages leading up to puberty in order to explain the body.

The Bible makes it clear that *sexual intimacy* is a gift to be enjoyed only within the ***marriage covenant between a husband and***

wife. The Bible warns against sex outside the husband-wife relationship. Yet, the need to experience sexual intimacy is a natural and powerful drive for young people. Television, movies, the internet, and social media present sexual temptations that earlier generations did not have to confront. That, coupled with intense peer pressure, makes it extremely challenging for a teenager to make healthy choices when it comes to sexuality.

Recognize that your teenager will make his or her own value decisions regarding sexuality and other topics. Your primary role as a parent is not to control your teen's every action but to influence his or her heart so he or she makes Godly choices.

You can be proactive in talking to your teen about sexuality when he or she begins showing interest in the opposite sex by having a *Key Talk*. Take your teenager out for a meal at a special restaurant of his or her choice. It is usually best to enjoy the meal in the middle of the afternoon, when the restaurant is somewhat empty to allow for a better discussion. After the meal, discuss four topics:

1. The Biblical view of marriage
2. The benefits of waiting until marriage for sexual intimacy
3. The importance of setting healthy limits to avoid temptation
4. Sexually transmitted diseases

Always ensure that this *Key Talk* is a time of listening with "How" and "What" questions. Some examples of "How" and "What" questions are:

- What are some ideas from the Bible regarding marriage?
- What are the benefits of waiting until marriage for sexual intimacy?
- How can establishing limits of what you will do or not do when dating often prevent problematic sexual activity?

- How frequently are STDs transmitted and what STDs may last a lifetime? Let your teen come up with the answers but be prepared to help with facts.

To assist you, I want to share the benefits of waiting for sexual intimacy until marriage. Those benefits are: no fear of sexually transmitted diseases, no fear of pregnancy, no comparison with one's spouse, joy over making the future marriage exclusive, growth in one's Christian walk, respect for self, respect for one's future spouse, making the honeymoon special, abstaining from sin, and no guilt before God.

During the *Key Talk,* don't talk too much and resist absolutely the temptation to lecture! Lecturing and moralizing will not be effective and may actually make sexual intimacy more appealing for your teenager. Stay out of power struggles and have a loving tone of voice that shows deep respect for your child's feelings and thoughts. When you communicate your values, make sure you do so clearly and respectfully recognize that sexual intimacy is a decision for your teenager.

Some parents establish a "virginity pact" or "virginity pledge" with their teen which is a wonderful idea. By agreeing to such a pact or pledge, a teenager promises to lead an abstinence-only lifestyle that honors God, respects self, and respects one's future spouse. It is important that the pact or pledge is not seen merely as a vehicle to appease parents, but as an opportunity to live as one who has been redeemed by Christ wanting to live a righteous life. In that sense, the promise is an oath also to God.

Should you choose to create a pact or pledge with your teen, I recommend that you make it concrete—and thus more likely to be achieved—by writing it on paper. Include the reasons and benefits of the agreement. Encourage your child to review it on a regular basis. Some parents have found that giving their son or daughter a ring, bracelet, or wristband is a helpful visual reminder.

Pray daily that your child will be wrapped in our Heavenly Father's loving arms and protected by His guardian angels from sexual abuse. Pray daily that your child will have wisdom and strength to resist sexual temptation. Finally, pray that God would lead your child to find a Christian spouse who is equally determined to respect *God's Gift Of Sex*.

85. Coping Skills for a Child with Anxiety and Depression

Children and teens experiencing anxiety and depression are on the rise and it is a serious problem. Books have been written on anxiety answers and depression solutions, so this lesson is just a brief overview. The Bible speaks of anxiety in several passages including Proverbs 12:25, "A person's anxiety will weigh him down, but an encouraging word makes him joyful" (GW) and again in 1 Peter 5:7, "Turn all your anxiety over to God because he cares for you" (GW).

Due to excessive technology use, social isolation and a lack of interaction among children is on the rise, which is also one reason for an increase in anxiety and depression. Many believers in the Bible like Elijah, David, Jonah, Jeremiah, Job, and Peter struggled with anxiety and depression that was heightened due to social isolation and lack of a support network.

Absolutely know that anxiety and depression are not an indication of weak Christian faith or fragile character.

Anxiety is an exaggerated emotional response versus a normal reaction to stress. Although those feelings are frightening, they are not dangerous. When a child is anxious it may be due to the words, actions, or non-actions of one parent or both parents. Due to one or both parents, the family atmosphere is not healthy and that often causes a child to feel anxious or depressed. I have counseled hundreds of anxious children. My initial goal is to help parents stop their unintentional unhealthy words and behaviors that make the anxiety even worse.

For example, I counseled a nine-year old girl whose parents frequently talked about being anxious and depressed over events in their personal lives. Remember children are emotional sponges. When their daughter experienced a stressful event, the parents exacerbated the problem by overly focusing on her anxious feelings. The mom had learned from another counselor to rate the anxiety from one to ten which can be an over focus on the anxiety. The result was that, frequently, their daughter was rating anxiety in her life with even minor worries. This nine-year old girl was constantly fearful, afraid to attempt almost any activity, and struggled in many areas of life.

In coping with anxiety, first and foremost, never use the words "anxious," "nervous," or "worried" in your life as a parent and encourage your child to do the same. In place of the words anxious and nervous use the word "***excited***." In place of the word worry use the word "***care***." Rather than saying "I am anxious" or "I am nervous" say "I am ***excited***." Rather than saying "I am worried" say, "I ***care***."

Many years ago, parents brought their ten-year old son to counseling because he was "so anxious, nervous, and worried," he could not attend school and had not done so the last two weeks. I found out that his parents used and stressed the words "anxious," "nervous," and "worried" every day.

I suggested to the ten-year old that he begin making statements like, "I am *excited* about school" and "I *care* about my math test." I will never forget his comment, "Dr. Schroeder that is giving a positive meaning to those dirty words and I like that." I responded with, "You said it much better than I and you are totally right." I am happy to write that this ten-year old went to school the very next day and his anxiety began to diminish. The "dirty words" were also dropped from the family vocabulary.

High expectations can be overwhelming, create anxiety, and often are the result of using the words "should," "must," "have to," and "ought to." In place of those absolutes, your child will benefit from "***I wish***" and "***It would be nice.***" For example, "I *wish* I would do well on my spelling test" or "It *would be nice* to enjoy school tomorrow," rather than "I must do well" or "I should enjoy school." Relieve daily pressure for your child by implementing a new way of speaking with "*I wish*" and "*It would be nice.*"

A child or adult saying the following three meaningful phrases out loud may also diminish anxiety, "*I am safe,*" "*God is with me,*" "*Jesus lives in me.*" Have your child picture his or her safest place on earth, the inside of church, the family living room, lying in bed under the covers, etc. and then say out loud, "*I am safe.*"

Then, have your child visualize God wrapping him or her in His loving arms and state out loud, "*God is with me.*"

Finally, confidently know that Jesus lives in your child, as expressed in Galatians 2:20, "Christ lives in me." So have your child say out loud "*Jesus lives in me.*" I recommend that your child close his or her eyes, picture those images, and say that mantra consecutively three times out loud. This is not a magical wand, but it can make a difference. A depressed child is seeking hope and looking for a sunrise in life, and those three statements may help.

I refer to anxiety and depression as first cousins because a child or person often has both at the same time. A few of the reasons for depression are dysfunctional thinking, significant losses, guilt, hopelessness, helplessness, and low self-worth. Please note that once a child or any person becomes depressed, he or she usually behaves in a way that reinforces the depression.

A key phrase to combat depression is, "*Do* my way to feeling better and do not try to think my way to happiness." Taking an active approach often develops hope. Of course, hope begins and ends in Jesus, so prayer, devotions, and worship are important. Shown below are ten practical suggestions to help a child cope with depression.

1. A parent needs to give significant verbal reassurance like compliments and praise.

2. Go for a walk, a bike ride, or just do any form of physical activity to overcome the emotional paralysis that often creates a passivity to do nothing.
3. Brighten your home because light combats the darkness of depression.
4. "Stay out of jail" which means do not let your child socially isolate, detaching himself or herself from the family or staying in the bedroom or home for lengthy periods of time. Avoiding every form of social isolation is a must!
5. Watch comedy television or movies because laughter releases the feel-good brain chemical called endorphins.
6. Have your child take a bath or shower every day because that provides a feeling of washing away the negative emotions.
7. Help your child avoid all-or-nothing thinking by expecting a "B-" or an 80 percent day. Every day is not either totally good or totally bad. Good things and not-so-good things happen on a daily basis for everyone.
8. Daily have your child accomplish one small chore or task to build self-worth.
9. Touch helps a child emotionally! Provide substantial daily physical affection.
10. A person is happy when he or she sings, but he or she can also sing to become happy. Have your child sing or hum a joyful song to help him or her feel happy.

There are no simple answers with anxiety and depression. If there were simple solutions very few people would be anxious and depressed. Yet, I have witnessed these suggestions helping numerous children and adults with anxiety and depression. If necessary, seek outside help for your child like your pediatrician or a competent counselor who understands and respects your Biblical beliefs.

CHAPTER 7

HABITS THAT STRENGTHEN FAITH

The Bible declares, "Children are a gift from the Lord; they are a reward from him" (Psalm 127:3 NLT). Jesus blessed little children and spoke about how special they were to Him in the Gospel of Mark, "People were bringing children to Him (Jesus) so that He would touch and bless them . . . He said to them (the disciples), 'Allow the children to come to Me; do not forbid them; for the kingdom of God belongs to such as these'" (Mark 10:13-14 AMP).

The most important thing in life is for your child to know that through faith in Jesus, the Savior of the world, there is everlasting life in heaven. Faith always comes first in a Christian home as Psalm 127:1 declares, "Unless the Lord builds the house, the builders labor in vain" (NIV). Experience Christ's love within your family through worship, prayer, devotions, and Bible reading. The purpose of this chapter is to assist you and your child with growing in faith, as well as communicating to your child your desire for his or her eternal well-being in heaven. Daily help your child understand what it means to have faith in Jesus.

86. Discussions About Eternal Life in Heaven

Jesus is our entire life not just on earth but for everlasting life in heaven! As a Christian parent, your main objective is to help your child understand that the crucifixion and resurrection are inseparable victories which together form the eternal hope of every Christian. Our mortal life is nothing more than a blink of the eye compared to eternity. All that truly matters after this earthly life is that your child is with you in the mansions of heaven forevermore.

Many Christians do not understand what it means to have eternal life in heaven. The goal of this lesson is to briefly explain faith in Jesus and eternal life in heaven by sharing the basics in order to provide you with knowledge that can be regularly discussed with your child.

Jesus Christ is the only way to heaven. Many people believe in works righteousness, which means being a good person opens the door to heaven. However, no one can earn even a tiny room in heaven through good works or being a nice person. Eternal life in heaven is a free gift from God through one's faith in Jesus Christ. "For God so loved the world that He gave His one and only Son, that whoever believes in Him shall not perish but have eternal life (in heaven)" (John 3:16 NIV).

Eternal life is being with Almighty God forevermore. Jesus said to the thief on the cross, "Today you will be with me in Paradise" (Luke 23:43 NIV). Just like the thief on the cross, at the very moment of our death, we are in the presence of our loving God in heaven. Job says, "After my skin has been destroyed, yet in my flesh I will see God" (Job 19:26 NIV). In I Thessalonians 4:17, the Bible says, "Then, together with them, we who are still alive and remain on the earth will be caught up in the clouds to meet the Lord in the air. Then we will be with the Lord forever" (NLT).

Heaven is a wonderful place of splendor and beauty. Jesus said, "I go to *prepare a place* for you, I will come again. Then I will bring you into my presence so that you will be where I am"

(John 14:3 GW). Please read Revelation 21:11-27 to fully understand the exquisite grandeur and magnificence of heaven, simply a beautiful place!

Our bodies, not just our souls, will be in heaven. Philippians 3:21 joyfully declares, "Who, by exerting that power which enables Him (Jesus) even to subject everything to Himself, will [not only] transform [but completely refashion] our *earthly* bodies so that they will be like His glorious *resurrected* body" (AMP). And further evidence is found in I Corinthians 15:20, "But now [as things really are] Christ has *in fact* been raised from the dead, [and He became] the first fruits [that is, the first to be resurrected with an incorruptible, immortal body, foreshadowing the resurrection] of those who have fallen asleep [in death]" (AMP). 1 Corinthians 15:52 also affirms, "For a trumpet will sound, and the dead [who believed in Christ] will be raised imperishable, and we will be [completely] changed [wondrously transformed]" (AMP). With confidence, know fully that our bodies will be perfect without any flaws in heaven.

There will be only joy and happiness in heaven. Revelation 7:16 states, "Never again will they hunger; never again will they thirst. The sun will not beat upon them, nor any scorching heat" (NIV). And again, in Revelation 21:4, "He (God) will wipe away every tear from their eyes. There will be no more death or mourning or crying or pain, for the old order of things has passed away" (NIV).

You and your child will know everyone in heaven including family members, friends, and all believers. You can find great joy in the thought of a remarkable reunion with our loved ones in heaven forevermore! Luke 9:30 confirms the fact of knowing everyone, "Two men, Moses and Elijah, appeared in glorious splendor, talking with Jesus" (NIV). And Jesus said, "I say to you that many will come from the east and the west, and will take their places at the feast with Abraham, Isaac and Jacob in the kingdom of heaven" (NIV). You and your child, along with all the saints, can take sweet comfort realizing that believers will know loved ones and all believers from the time of Adam and Eve.

Eternity is unending life. The debt of the United States is trillions of dollars, a number truly beyond our comprehension. If you live to a hundred, that seems like a very long time, but our earthly life is nothing more than a blink of the eye. Eternal life is even more than trillions times a hundred years. Our heavenly home will last forever and ever!!! Thus, all that really matters for your child and every person is eternal life in heaven with our loving God.

I pray this brief description of faith in Jesus, along with an explanation of what eternal life in heaven will be like, will enhance your ongoing discussions with your child. I encourage you to have fun talking with your child about heavenly things like streets lined with gold, who you would like to talk to, the kind of mansion you want in heaven, etc. My wife and I have thoroughly enjoyed those discussions with our grandchildren.

87. The Apologizing and Forgiving Process

An unfortunate reality is that parents and their children are imperfect, flawed individuals who will make mistakes. As with all relationships, forgiveness is the glue that restores brokenness back together again. James 5:16 encourages, "Therefore, confess your sins to one another and pray for one another, that you may be healed" (ESV) and that includes both parents and children.

Christianity is appropriately called the Good News of Forgiveness. However, most people are practically unaware of how to apologize and forgive. After researching and then writing my 350-page doctoral dissertation on this subject, I am thoroughly convinced every satisfying relationship, including parent-child, always has apologizing and forgiving at the heart.

Parents are to be the examples whenever they are at fault to demonstrate how to apologize and request forgiveness. A child learns more quickly by observing how his or her parent apologizes and seeks forgiveness.

I passionately believe a child will be more emotionally healthy as an adult when he or she has parents who are willing to admit their wrongs. Parents who model the forgiveness process demonstrate what provides a fresh start for every relationship. A child then grows up comprehending that perfection is an unachievable goal because even mom and dad make mistakes. A child is also more able to give himself or herself grace and mercy for being imperfect.

There are five aspects of the apologizing and forgiving process which are shown below.

1. ***Regret***. Regret is a feeling of sadness at having committed a wrong. However, there is no mental promise to not commit that mistake again because it is just a whimsical wish.
2. ***Repentance***. Repentance is one step beyond regret and a mental pledge to make a total behavioral change in order to never commit that wrong again.
3. ***Apologizing***. An apology requires courage and happens through the statement, "I am sorry I hurt you by . . ." I think it is especially important to use the word "hurt" to indicate compassion for what the other person felt from the wrong.
4. ***Humility***. It necessitates humility to ask, "Will you please forgive me?" Using the word "will" implies commitment and the word "please" is essential for kindness.
5. ***Forgiveness***. A proper response is, "I forgive you," which heals the relationship. The word "forgive" should always be used and not just say, "That's okay" or "No problem" or "I'm over it."

One of the most important life lessons a child can learn is how to apologize and forgive. Shown below is how the three-step process works when a child makes a mistake.

1. ***Apologizing***. "Mom and dad, I am sorry I hurt you by being disrespectful."
2. ***Humility***. "Will you please forgive me?"
3. ***Forgiveness***. "We forgive you."

Certainly, when necessary, a parent needs to apologize to his or her child as well. Forgiveness is truly at the heart of a parent-child relationship.

When one sibling hurts another in any way, parents often request that the offender apologize to the offended *but* the humility part of "*Will you please forgive me?*" is often omitted. Unfortunately, many people, including most parents, do not know the three-step process but now you have that knowledge.

If a child only has to say, "I am sorry," the apology is often flippant and insincere. The humility component is critical because it teaches and creates the compassionate repentance that must always be present. In addition, when the offended party completes the process with, "*I forgive you,*" it heals the relationship.

I was a seminary professor for almost twenty-five years and taught future pastors the apologizing and forgiving process in various counseling classes. Hundreds of seminarians reported that they were extremely happy and amazed how their children's relationships immensely improved when they learned the complete three-step process. Before gaining this knowledge, the future pastors reported they only had their children say, "I am sorry . . ." The critical changes were "***Will you please forgive me?***" and "***I forgive you***."

The Bible has nearly 125 references to the importance of forgiveness for interpersonal relationships. One of the most important interpersonal relationships is the parent-child. Perhaps the greatest life skill that a parent must teach a child is the ***apologizing and forgiving process***. If you would like a more detailed explanation and understanding of *Apologizing and Forgiving* please read chapter one of the Christian marriage book, ***Simple Habits for Marital Happiness***, written by this author.

88. A Church for Worship

As a Christian parent, your first priority is to regularly communicate faith to your child for his or her eternal well-being. That is accomplished best by being a role model in all areas of life as 1 Timothy 4:12 declares, "Make your speech, behavior, love, faith, and purity an example for other believers" (GW). One way to be an example is through prioritizing worship just as the Bible encourages, "Young men and women, old and young together. Let them praise the name of the Lord because his name is high above all others. His glory is above heaven and others" (Psalm 148:12-13 GW). As you *train* (Proverbs 22:6) your child, place a high priority on weekly or at least regular worship.

Due to our mobile society, finding the right church has become a common occurrence because of the frequency of moving. There are many Christian denominations, so attempt to choose a church that clearly teaches the truth about God and Biblical beliefs. Selecting a Biblically-based church may be a challenge since Godly values are declining. For the sake of consistency, parents need to agree together on one church that best exposes their child to our loving God in Jesus. Attending two different churches easily confuses a child.

Hopefully, all family members can agree upon a church home, although parents will make the final decision. Before selecting a church, collect as much information as possible. When a church is Biblically-based, determine if the church agrees with your top priorities. Shown below are four criteria to consider:

1. *Opportunities.* Does the church have Sunday School classes, an active youth program, Bible-study groups, variety of service opportunities, etc.?
2. *Distance from your home.* Unfortunately, this may be a high priority because a lengthy drive can make a church unappealing for your child, especially a teenager.
3. *Style of worship.* Does the church provide both traditional and contemporary services? Some people, especially teens, do not prefer organ music but instead enjoy praising God with guitars, drums, keyboard, and a group of singers.
4. *Worship structure.* Some churches include children during the service while others encourage a child to grow in his or her faith with other children in a classroom.

Keep in mind, there is no perfect church or perfect pastor. Since a church consists of sinners, I think the best a church can be is a "B," so keep that reality in mind when selecting one for your child and you.

A Christian parent wants Jesus to be an important part of a child's life. Pray that God will grant you wisdom in selecting a church where you and your child can worship the one true God. If you are unable to worship weekly with your child, have a written goal or indicate on the family calendar when you plan to worship. Without an exact plan, worship can definitely become infrequent. At times you may not have enthusiasm to worship but still be a role model by joyfully attending church.

89. Connect Through Prayer

When a person believes in Jesus, prayer or talking daily to God is a normal response from the heart. Prayer is an expression of our faith and a precious blessing for our lives.

As individuals, Christians are encouraged to pray, but it is equally important for a parent and child to spend time together in prayer.

An essential thought is, "I will pray and keep on praying with my child!" 1 Thessalonians 5:16-18 confirms the importance of prayer and thanksgiving, "Always be joyful. *Never stop praying.* Whatever happens, give thanks, because it is God's will in Christ Jesus that you do this" (GW). Have the goals of praying often with your child and letting your child see you frequently praying.

A child may learn from your prayer life but, if necessary, teach your child how to pray. If you are not sure how to pray, organize your prayers into three parts. Prayers may be short and concise even focusing on only one specific idea or request.

The *first step* is to say something as simple as "Dear God" or "Loving God" or "Heavenly Father" or "Lord God." In the *second part,* have your child say one sentence that may express thankfulness, confess a sin, pray for others, pray for a particular personal need, share a specific burden, etc. If your child wants to say additional sentences, of course that is fine, but take the pressure off by suggesting one sentence. The *final part* is concluding "in Jesus name," because Jesus is the mediator between believers and our Heavenly Father by taking our prayers to God the Father.

An example prayer that your child might say is:

Dear God,
Thank you for blessing me with a good day at school.
In Jesus name. Amen.

At times, adults and children may not be sure what to pray for. The fingers on the hand can easily offer guidance and can be used daily for a prayer plan.

When holding up your hand with the palm facing out, the *thumb* is closest to the heart. The *thumb* reminds you to pray for those closest to your heart like family and friends.

The *pointing finger* includes people who point us in the right direction like teachers, pastors, doctors, and everyone who instructs.

The *tallest finger* stands for those in high authority like our leaders at the local, state, and national government level. Pray that government officials will lead based on God's guidance through Biblical principles.

The *ring finger* is the weakest prompting us to pray for those who are sick, have troubling circumstances, or are in any kind of pain.

Finally, the *little finger* is the smallest and reminds your child to pray for his or her own needs.

Using the hand as a prayer guide has been around forever but is greatly beneficial.

A believer's prayer life is far too often neglected and viewed as a last resort only when a crisis arises. Teach your child to start the day in prayer and end the day with prayer. Here are some other times to pray: before taking a trip, mealtimes, doing homework, studying for a test, facing a life challenge, coping with a health issue, experiencing sad situations, etc.

We are focusing on our loving God's continued blessings when prayers are said before and after meals. You can find many prayer examples by searching the internet. A couple of pre-meal prayers are: "God is great, and God is good, Let us thank Him for our food. In Jesus' name, Amen" and "Come Lord Jesus be our guest, let your gifts to us be blessed. Amen." An after-meal example is: "O give thanks unto God for He is good, and His love endures forever. Amen."

When it is a common prayer, include your child by letting him or her begin the mealtime prayer, or if there is more than one child, then alternate who starts the prayer. It is not necessary to always use a traditional mealtime prayer, but at times, offer an extemporaneous prayer either by a parent or the child.

Prayer is effective and a powerful connection to God. Pray with your child on a daily basis, watch your parent-child relationship grow over time, and be encouraged by your child's Christian walk. After praying often with your child, hopefully "talking to God" will become a comfortable experience and happen daily.

90. Family Devotions

A parent has a responsibility to keep Jesus at the center of the family. One of the best ways to do that is through family devotions. Maybe you have never tried having devotions in your home. If that is the case, recognize time together focusing on God is all important when it comes to leading and guiding your child.

It takes time to adjust to any new family activity, even devotions, but it will happen! A family spending time together focusing on God will create a safe, secure feeling in a child's heart.

Every Christian home will benefit immensely from regular devotions. Through devotions a child learns the love of God, while at the same time receiving love from his or her parents. Amazing things happen when parents and their children have frequent devotions. Devotions help family members grow together while faith in Jesus is also strengthened.

Consistency

Have a main goal to meaningfully connect with each other and God in the midst of a busy life. There is a tremendous benefit in gathering as a family to discuss faith in Jesus, eternal life in heaven, and life values based on the Bible. If you have never had devotions together, it is usually better to begin with brief ones.

Make them enjoyable and watch your tone of voice because that will determine the devotional atmosphere. Hence, your tone needs to be joyful and encouraging, not serious and grim. The goal is for your child to look forward to enjoying devotions.

It is also not the *how* that is important, but the *do* with family devotions. Be intentional and faithful with your devotions. Do not set your standards too high or be too demanding, instead aim for regular occurrences. Expect there will be more days when devotions do not happen but avoid being discouraged by looking forward to the next opportunity. As a parent, give yourself grace and mercy realizing that three days per week is a realistic goal.

Have a plan and pick a devotion time that works best for your family. Choose a time during the day when the family is most unhurried. Dinner time and bedtime are often traditional favorites, but due to busy schedules, other times may be more convenient. Turn off all electronics. Have a routine so everyone knows what to expect with devotion time.

You want devotions to be a relaxed family time of growing in faith. Location is just as important as time. Perhaps, have devotions in various places from time to time for a pleasant change of scenery like the kitchen table, patio, living room, bedroom, in a circle on a rug, sitting in lawn chairs outside, the front porch, etc.

Simple Format

On the internet, you can find devotional books for all ages, picture Bibles, storybook Bibles, and age-appropriate devotional books. Other possibilities for devotional resources are your church denomination's online bookstore, Christianbook.com, and FocusOnTheFamily.com.

Devotions are not a church service with rigid structure, but a time to place God at the center of the family in an easygoing, laidback way. Casual conversations are opportunities to talk about your faith journey. Keep it simple by having the basic ingredients the same:

- Devotional reading or Bible story
- Ask "How" and "What" questions about the reading or Bible story
- Conclude with prayer

Take turns reading the devotion or Bible story. Get every family member involved by asking age-appropriate questions to engage your child. Conclude with a prayer and when possible hold hands because touch emotionally connects you.

Be Brief

One key to family devotions is briefness! Attention spans are sometimes short especially with younger children. Active minds tend to wander so keep devotions brief.

By keeping it short, I am suggesting less than five minutes, but be flexible. It is often best to conclude the devotion when a child's interest is high. The most meaningful conversations happen when a child wants to freely keep talking rather than being forced.

Persistence Is Important

A time of meaningful family devotions requires patience and perseverance. If your family is like most, you may find it difficult to get together for devotions, thus, be persistent with your effort. Besides a parent's hectic schedule, a child has homework, friends, and numerous other activities.

Perhaps, ask other parents how they make their devotion time valuable and workable. Devotions are a great way for you and your child to talk about our Savior, Jesus Christ. Always know and believe that God will richly bless your family as you grow together in your faith in Jesus through devotions.

No matter how infrequently it happens, God is blessing your family devotional time! Never be discouraged and stick with the plan!

CONCLUSION

I hope and pray you are confidently optimistic that you can lead your child to one day become a self-assured, self-reliant, and responsible adult. Daily strive to influence your child's heart with this wonderful parenting knowledge. Refer to this comprehensive guidebook often by rereading it over and over to reinforce the skills and tools you now possess.

Be patient, go slow, and lower your expectations!

Give yourself grace and mercy recognizing there is no ideal, perfect parent. Applying these skills and knowledge will strengthen your competence and enjoyment in *effectively parenting* your child.

No two parents are alike nor does every parenting idea make sense for both mom and dad. However, I pray reading this excellent resource together will help both parents mutually agree on how to effectively influence their child's heart. The mother of all learning is repetition. Thus, both parents applying this knowledge in the exact same way will have a significant positive impact on a child.

For encouragement and positive reinforcement, perhaps start a parenting support group at church, your neighborhood, with other friends, MOPS moms, etc. It might be beneficial to download the FREE Discussion Guide for ***Effective Parenting*** at CrossLinkPublishing.com as a resource for your weekly, biweekly, or monthly meetings. For inspiration and motivation, it could also be helpful to have a regular accountability checkup with another same-sex parent who has also read ***Simple Habits for Effective Parenting***.

Implementing these successful skills, strategies, and tools will help you confidently trust in your abilities to lovingly lead and guide your child. You may or may not witness immediate results, but I truly believe you will notice a positive difference in your child's attitude, words, and behaviors.

My fervent prayer is that through ***Simple Habits for Effective Parenting*** your child will become a happy, confident, responsible, Godly adult one day. You can now say, "I have kept the faith in leading my child and I can hear God speaking to me, 'Well done good and faithful parent.'"

ABOUT THE AUTHOR

Dr. Randy Schroeder is the author of the three-time national award-winning marriage book, *Simple Habits For Marital Happiness*. He is an enthusiastic speaker who is motivated to enhance the lives of others. For more than four decades through his speaking and counseling, Dr. Schroeder has thoroughly enjoyed educating parents and enriching couples' relationships with commonsense wisdom.

He holds a Ph.D. in Marriage and Family Therapy, a Master of Divinity, and Master of Education in Administration. Dr. Schroeder is a former seminary professor of Pastoral Counseling where he taught classes on the Christian family, marriage, premarital preparation, crisis counseling, and more.

Dr. Schroeder has a successful counseling practice in Carmel, Indiana, and is passionate about helping parents, couples, and individuals achieve satisfying lives and relationships.

Randy and his wife, Ginny, have been married for over forty-five years, have two married sons, six grandchildren, and reside in the Indianapolis area.

For more information regarding Dr. Schroeder and his speaking availability, you may contact him through DrRandySchroeder.com.

Printed in the United States
by Baker & Taylor Publisher Services